REPRESENTATIVE AMERICAN SPEECHES 1977-1978

edited by WALDO W. BRADEN
Boyd Professor of Speech
Louisiana State University

THE REFERENCE SHELF
Volume 50 Number 4

THE H. W. WILSON COMPANY
New York 1978

THE REFERENCE SHELF

The books in this series contain reprints of articles, excerpts from books, and addresses on current issues and social trends in the United States and other countries. There are six separately bound numbers in each volume, all of which are generally published in the same calendar year. One number is a collection of recent speeches; each of the others is devoted to a single subject and gives background information and discussion from various points of view, concluding with a comprehensive bibliography. Books in the series may be purchased individually or on subscription.

Library of Congress Catalog Card
Representative American speeches, 1937/38–
New York, H. W. Wilson Co.
v. 21. cm. annual. (The Reference shelf)
Editors: 1937/38–1958/59, A. C. Baird.–1959/60–1969/70. L. Thonssen.–1970/71– W. W. Braden.
I. American orations. 2. Speeches, addresses, etc.
I. Baird, Albert Craig, ed. II. Thonssen, Lester, ed. III. Braden, Waldo W., ed. IV. Series.
PS668.B3 815.5082 38–27962

International Standard Book Number 0–8242–0625–8
PRINTED IN THE UNITED STATES OF AMERICA

PREFACE

OVERVIEW OF PUBLIC ADDRESS, 1977-1978

The year 1977-1978 was a quiet one. Compared to recent years, it was far less dramatic in happenings and failed to stir much notable eloquence in public address. Of course, nothing during the twelve months could approach the excitement of such events as Watergate, the fall of Richard M. Nixon, and the dramatic electoral victories of Jimmy Carter. Even the stirring moments of the Bicentennial had largely disappeared from the scene.

Public address during the year concentrated primarily upon matters of domestic concern: ratification of the treaties with Panama, inflation, energy, pollution, education, the future of the humanities and arts. The Carter Administration necessarily devoted thought and effort to foreign affairs: peace talks in the Middle East, the turmoil in Africa, relations with Latin America, and the SALT negotiations with the Soviet Union. President Carter's two trips overseas—the first, in January, to eastern Europe and Asia and the second, in March, to South America and Africa—demonstrated his eagerness to bolster the American image abroad. But at home and abroad he put more effort into symbolic gestures and quiet diplomacy than into dramatic rhetoric.

The media have had difficulty interpreting the Carter Administration. What is the real Carter? One reporter spoke of "his deliberately understated approach, a refreshing departure from traditional bombast and hyperbole of American politics" (James T. Wooten, New York *Times,* January 26, 1978). "All the adjectives and phrases people use to describe how Mr. Carter seems on one-to-one basis or in a small group include calm and relaxed, low keyed, a good listener, no theatrics, sincere, humble, charming. A reporter . . . says he makes you feel that you're the most important person in the world to him" (David Ensor, *Christian Science Monitor,* February 10, 1978).

Some observers of the politcial scene have wondered if Jimmy Carter is not the first television President. Does his informality, his low-keyed speaking, his sensitivity to image-building, his seeking of casual encounters, give him an edge in television appearances? Certainly John F. Kennedy, Lyndon B. Johnson, and Richard M. Nixon appeared often on television, but by their demeanor they sometimes appeared forced, aggressive, and too eager to sound eloquent. They had difficulty shaking off a style developed before live audiences that required an extended projection of tone and action. At times, in press conferences, close-in camera shots caught them in awkward grimaces or embarrassing responses that betrayed almost subliminal feelings that could evoke negative reactions from television viewers. President Carter has realized that what he does (his symbols) and how he appears may get a more lasting response than what he says. Thus, an overnight stay in a citizen's home may be more important than the actual speech he makes at the town meeting.

The ratification of the treaties with Panama brought sustained interest from June until the second vote was taken April 18, 1978. The "new right" organizations, supported by veterans' groups, and other conservatives conducted a massive media and lobbying campaign in opposition to ratification of the treaties. Ronald Reagan, former governor of California, was in the vanguard, speaking often. (His activities suggested that he may have had the presidential campaign of 1980 in mind.) The pro-treaty forces were more modest in their efforts, but President Carter directed his supporters, cabinet members, and others to take to the platform. On February 1, Carter explained the treaties in a fireside chat. The Administration efforts were centered on intense personal lobbying of the senators, who finally supported ratification of the treaties 68 to 32 on both votes (*Newsweek,* February 13, 1978, p 18-20).

The formal debate in the United States Senate lasted for eight weeks, with many senators participating. Included in this volume are speeches by S. I. Hayakawa (Republican, California), Daniel P. Moynihan (Democrat, New York), Orrin Hatch (Republican, Utah), and Thomas J. McIntyre (Democrat, New Hampshire). The McIntyre speech, called "one of the strongest speeches" heard in Congress "for some time" (Richard L. Strout, *Christian Science Monitor,* March 10, 1978), was probably the most memorable one of the debate. The Senate debate over the treaties with Panama was similar in some aspects to the one in 1918-1920 over whether this country should join the League of Nations, although no senator today can bring to the debate the same fiery rhetoric that William E. Borah of Idaho brought to the Senate in his opposition to the League.

Throughout the year the members of the President's cabinet and his staff have spoken frequently on a variety of issues, but none of their speeches, except that of Joseph Califano, Jr., Secretary of Health, Education, and Welfare, has stirred much excitement. The quiet style of Secretary of State Cyrus Vance, who has engaged in restrained and subdued diplomacy, contrasts with the flair of his predecessor, Henry A. Kissinger. Vice President Mondale has represented the Administration often and well, but he has never forgotten his subordinate role.

The new restrictions on what senators may earn on the lecture trail are beginning to affect their itinerating. At present, a senator is limited to an outside income from lecturing of $25,000, with no more than $2,000 per appearance. Thirty-six senators exceeded that last amount in 1976-1977. In the year prior to entering the Senate (1976), Senator Moynihan made more than $160,000 from his speeches (New York *Times,* April 20, 1977) and received between $3,000 and $5,000 per appearance. Samuel I. Hayakawa (Republican, California), Edmund Muskie (Democrat, Maine), and other senators say that they cannot maintain themselves in Washington, D.C. without substantial outside earnings. Five Republican senators, led by Paul Laxalt (Nevada) plan to challenge the limitations on outside income in court

(Walter R. Mears, Memphis *Press Scimitar,* August 17, 1977).

Some of the most memorable events of 1977-1978 were connected with the return to the Senate of Hubert H. Humphrey (Democrat, Minnesota), who was battling terminal cancer. His welcome in the Senate and subsequent appearances before his death elicited moving rhetoric. Putting aside political differences and personal rivalries, so prevalent in Washington, senators, high government officials, former Presidents and presidential aspirants poured forth admiration and respect for Humphrey. James P. Gannon put it well as follows: "Seldom has Washington witnessed a gathering of the past, present, and future generations of American leaders whose lives were individually and profoundly influenced by one man. The senator from Minnesota, bridging US political life from Franklin Roosevelt to Jimmy Carter, brought them all together one last time" (*Wall Street Journal,* January 16, 1978).

I am most grateful to many persons who have forwarded materials, answered my queries, supplied background information, made speech evaluations, and helped me assemble the volume. As usual, my colleagues in the department of speech at Louisiana State University have often come to my assistance. I appreciate the support that John H. Pennybacker, my departmental chairman, has given me. Mary Louise Gehring of Baylor University, Mary Margaret Roberts of Pittsburg (Kansas) State University, Richard L. Johannesen of Northern Illinois University, Ruth Ulman of The H. W. Wilson Company, and Carson Killen of Washington, D.C., have made suggestions concerning speeches. My secretary Virginia Steely and my research assistant Patricia Webb Robinson have always been most helpful. I appreciate the contributions of these persons and many others.

WALDO W. BRADEN

August, 1978
Baton Rouge, Louisiana

CONTENTS

DEBATE OVER THE PANAMA CANAL

FOR RATIFICATION OF TREATIES WITH PANAMA [1]

DEAN RUSK [2]

The new Panama Canal agreement, thirteen years in negotiation, is made up of two treaties; the first provides the timetable for transferring the canal and the Canal Zone to Panamanian control by the year 2000 and the second is to assure the permanent neutrality of the canal. Negotiated by Ellsworth Bunker and Sol M. Linowitz, the accords were signed by President Carter and the Panamanian leader, Brigadier General Omar Torrijos, in Washington, D. C., on September 7, 1977.

During the fall of 1977, the Senate Foreign Relations Committee held hearings on the proposed treaties with Panama. The committee, under the chairmanship of John Sparkman (Democrat, Alabama), was made up of sixteen members: ten Democrats and six Republicans. Among the committee members were many prominent senators. Democratic members included Frank Church (Idaho), Claiborne Pell (Rhode Island), George S. McGovern (South Dakota), Hubert H. Humphrey (Minnesota), Dick Clark (Iowa), Joseph R. Biden, Jr. (Delaware), John Glenn (Ohio), Richard Stone (Florida), and Paul S. Sarbanes (Maryland); Republican members included Clifford P. Case (New Jersey), Jacob K. Javits (New York), James B. Pearson (Kansas), Charles H. Percy (Illinois), Robert P. Griffin (Michigan), and Howard H. Baker, Jr. (Tennessee).

The committee held hearings in its own conference room. The members were seated at a long table in the front of the room facing the witnesses and the audience. The room seats about one hundred people. Those witnesses called to give testimony sit at small tables directly in front of the committee members, while the spectators sit farther back.

On October 14, 1977, the committee heard testimony in support of the treaties from two former secretaries of state of previous

[1] A statement presented to the US Senate Foreign Relations Committee meeting in Room 4221, Dirksen Senate Office Building, October 14, 1977. From the *Congressional Record,* October 17, 1977, p S17219–20.

[2] For biographical note, see Appendix.

administrations: Dean Rusk and Henry A. Kissinger. It also heard statements from Robert Charles Smith, national commander, the American Legion; Frank D. Ruggiero, national commander, AMVETS; Major General J. Milnor Roberts, USAR, executive director, Reserve Officers Association; and Colonel Phelps Jones (USA-Ret.), director, National Security and Foreign Affairs, Veterans of Foreign Wars.

Given here is the statement of Dean Rusk, who served in the Department of State in various positions during the Truman Administration from 1947 to 1951 and as secretary of state under Presidents Kennedy and Johnson, 1961-1969. As would be expected, his words carried considerable weight with the Senate committee. The soft-spoken Rusk read his carefully prepared statement, a fitting introduction to the case for ratification. Although he was seated and appearing before a Senate committee, he was making effective use of public address.

Mr. Chairman and distinguished Senators:

I am very glad to be here this morning to express my views on the Panama Treaties now pending before you. I am especially glad to be here with my distinguished friend Mr. Henry Kissinger. The fact that we are here together is a reminder that four presidents and four secretaries of state, of both political parties, have been closely involved in the negotiations which have led to the documents now before you for your consideration under the Constitution. Other presidents in this post-war period have also felt the pressures for a change in the status quo originated by the Treaty of 1903.

My remarks will be relatively brief and will consist of two or three main considerations which led me to support the proposed Treaties with Panama. Since you are exercising a solemn constitutional responsibility, you will necessarily go into every aspect of these treaties in great detail but as a private citizen, I propose simply to point to those aspects of the problem which seem to me to be decisive in forming my own opinion.

I begin with the conviction that the Treaty of 1903, as amended, offers a very fragile platform on which to try to stand in these closing decades of the twentieth century. In the mid-1960's, during and after the tragic riots in Panama, it became apparent to us that history had overtaken the status quo in Panama and that a new relationship would have to be found if our vital interests in the operation and safety of the canal were to be assured. Here I do not rest upon the murky circumstances surrounding the secession of Panama from Colombia and the conclusion of the treaty with Mr. Bunau-Varilla, a citizen of France with uncertain credentials as a representative of Panama. It is a fascinating story with a colorful cast of characters. But I see little point in our now wearing sack cloth and ashes over what our grandfathers did in another historical era, when what happened in most of the world was determined by decisions made or not made in a handful of western capitals. We should not, however, be under the illusion that those events could stand the test of modern standards of treaty making.

The 1903 Treaty seemed to me to take its place alongside the so-called "unequal" treaties which certain western powers imposed upon China in the nineteenth century and the Capitulations which gave certain powers extraterritorial rights in the Ottoman Empire. Even if we had acquired absolute title to the Canal Zone, which we did not, the general international policy and practice of decolonization would have rendered the status quo in Panama untenable.

The Vienna Convention on the Law of Treaties is now pending before your committee and your action upon it has been delayed for reasons well known to you. I would suppose, however, that the contents of that convention already apply to the United States and to other nations since the convention simply codifies established rules of customary international law.

It seems to me that the 1903 Treaty with Panama is vulnerable to the doctrine of "fundamental change of circumstances" *(rebus sic stantibus)* found in Article 62 of the Convention. In my view, the United Nations Charter contains the overriding statement of international law and policy—despite our occasional irritations over the conduct of members in some organs of the UN organization itself and the many failures of members of the world community in giving effect to charter precepts. The charter insists upon the "sovereign equality of all its Members" (Article 2, paragraph 1) and calls for respect for "the equal rights . . . of nations large and small" (Preamble). I have already mentioned decolonization, well established both in principle and practice by the charter and by the history of this postwar era.

Treaties are the primary source of international law partly because they are drafted in relatively precise terms of legal obligation and, more importantly, because they represent the consent of the sovereign parties who agree to them. We can not seriously suggest that the 1903 Treaty represents the consent of Panama or of its people. It would be accurate to say that if the United States were a party to a treaty which became obnoxious to our public policy and repugnant to our people, we would move to denounce it and relieve ourselves of its burdens.

Article 64 of the Convention on the Law of Treaties states, "if a new preemptory norm of general international law emerges, any existing treaty which is in conflict with that norm becomes void and terminates." Lawyers have debated at considerable length this doctrine of "jus cogens" and the identity of the norms which can be said to be preemptory in character. They are probably few in number. I would suggest to you that, in the modern world, one nation can not maintain a presence within another nation without the consent of the second nation. If the situation in Eastern Europe is different, the contrast merely emphasizes the general rule and provides no precedent for the United States. We have withdrawn from valuable bases and installations in Libya, Ethiopia, and Pakistan; we have seen the use of bases in Turkey sharply restricted by that government; we withdrew our forces from France on the demand of President de Gaulle. I can imagine the astonishment on President de Gaulle's face had I been instructed to tell him that we could not withdraw our forces from France because their presence was covered by an agreement between our two countries. We know that such bases and personnel as we have in other countries require the consent of the governments concerned and that some of them have charged us very high prices for that consent. The 1903 Treaty with Panama is not an adequate substitute for such consent: it is not an arrangement which could be negotiated in this latter part of the twentieth century. I do not know whether President Theodore Roosevelt was accurately quoted in a remark about Panama: "We wanted it; we took it." But let us be under no illusion—an attempt to maintain our position in the Panama Canal Zone on the basis of the 1903 Treaty would be an act of force—as in Eastern Europe. We can choose that course if we are prepared to pay the heavy political, economic, and military costs involved.

In concluding my comment on the status of the 1903 Treaty, let me add that I do not believe that we could afford to allow the validity of that treaty to be tested in the International Court of Justice. I am glad that that treaty has not been pursued in the General Assembly of the United Nations where I would suspect we would be almost alone in the voting. Some of our closest friends would leave us because of considerations of general policy. When the United Nations Security Council met in Panama in 1973 and had before it a resolution on Panama, hostile to United States interests, it was necessary for our representative to exercise a veto, with no member of the Council voting with us. There were 13 "yes" votes, the UK abstained, and the United States cast the only negative vote. Close friends such as France, Australia, Austria, and Kenya voted against us.

An alternative is to try to safeguard our interests in the Panama Canal by agreement between ourselves and Panama in a modern setting. There are very strong feelings among the peoples of our two countries, feelings which make it very difficult for governments to find agreement with which all can be satisfied. These feelings will be further acerbated during the present debate in both countries about the new treaties; already what is said in one country is being used to inflame feelings in the other country. Opponents of these treaties object to our making such agreements with a dictator. Having been involved with this problem before the present regime in Panama came to power, I would suggest that the more democratic the government in Panama, the more insistent they would be on a prompt and fundamental change in the arrangements regarding the canal.

Our national interest lies in access to and the safety of the Panama Canal itself, not in a continuation of our special position in the Zone. I believe that our interest in the canal includes a residual responsibility to the maritime nations of the world and to certain nations of our own hemisphere for whom the canal is a life line. But surely we should attempt to satisfy these interests by agreement and should seek to engage the friendship and cooperation of the Panamanian government and people in the decades ahead. We can give ourselves a chance to repair the injuries we have inflicted upon national pride and individual dignity and proceed in the future on the basis that we and the Panamanians need each other in these matters.

We must take into account, however, the possibility that events will not work out as we now hope. Under the new treaties, we shall have twenty-three years to test the ability of Panama and ourselves to proceed on the basis of agreement. The responsibilities which we would have until the year 2000 clearly make it possible for us to insure the operation and safety of the canal. Beginning with the year 2000, questions regarding passage and safety of the canal would be governed by the provisions of the Treaty Concerning the Permanent Neutrality and Operation of the Panama Canal. Under Article IV of this treaty, "The United States of America and the Republic of Panama agree to maintain the regime of neutrality established in this Treaty." The joint responsibility of the United States and Panama for that "regime of neutrality" as spelled out in the treaty gives us, in my judgment, all that we need to maintain our essential interests in the matter, namely, passage and the security of the canal itself.

I am aware, Mr. Chairman, of the discussion which has occurred about whether Article IV of the Neutrality Treaty is understood in the same way by both ourselves and Panama and that discussions have been going on between Senators, the Executive Branch and Panama on that point. It would be inappropriate for me to inject myself into those discussions at this point. I might offer one observation, however, which may be relevant. I hope that we and Panama would not get tangled up with each other over the word "intervention." That is a word which has accumulated many barnacles over the years and carries with it memories which we ought to try to forget. What we are interested in is access to and the security of the Panama Canal. Measures to assure its passage and safety do not mean interference in the internal affairs of Panama.

In any event, I do not believe that we should approach such matters in terms of the worst case imaginable but rather through a genuine desire and expectation to work things out on an amicable basis. Providence has not given us the ability to pierce the fog of the future with accuracy and the year 2000 is a long way off. Perhaps we should not, today, try to answer every problem which might be posed to some future President and Congress. I must confess, however, that Article IV of the Neutrality Treaty played a major role in my own decision to support these two treaties. If, God forbid, it should ever become necessary for a President and a Congress to take strong measures to keep the canal functioning and safe, they would be in a far stronger position to do so under the Treaties of 1977 than under the anachronistic Treaty of 1903.

Thus, whether we are thinking of the principles upon which we hope to see a cooperative community of nations move into the future or are thinking about a hardheaded approach to adverse contingencies which may lurk in the future, it seems to me to be to our advantage to give effect to these two new treaties. The consequences of not doing so could be very severe. I see no point in inviting these consequences upon ourselves now when we have a good chance to avoid them altogether.

SENATE DEBATE OVER RATIFICATION OF TREATIES CONCERNING THE PANAMA CANAL [3]

SAMUEL I. HAYAKAWA, ORRIN G. HATCH, AND DANIEL P. MOYNIHAN [4]

The issue of the Panama Canal was an emotional one. In Latin America, the fifty-one-mile-long waterway stood as a hated symbol of Yankee imperialism. Remembering how it had been "hacked out of the jungle by thousands of men who braved and often succumbed to malaria and yellow fever," Americans thought of it as a symbol of Yankee enterprise and greatness. In the 1976 presidential campaign, Ronald Reagan, former governor of California, made an effective issue of canal negotiations in the Republican primary contest with Gerald Ford. Hardening his opposition, the former California governor stumped the country during the fall of 1977 and the spring of 1978 in an effort to strengthen resistance to ratification of the two treaties. He declared them a "risk . . . for our national security and for hemisphere defense." Representative John Murphy (Democrat, New York) feared that ratification would mean the "surrender of American-owned property in Panama to a revolutionary despot" (*Newsweek,* August 22, 1977, p 28-31; September 19, 1977, p 46-8).

Support for ratification came from both sides of the aisle in the Senate and was backed by leaders of past Republican Administrations, including former President Gerald Ford and former Secretary of State Henry A. Kissinger, as well as the Joint Chiefs of Staff.

The Carter Administration gave top priority to gaining ratification of the treaties with Panama, negotiated between February and August 1977, by two American diplomats, Ellsworth P. Bunker and Sol M. Linowitz. In June 1977, the Carter team initiated a campaign of education. The President met with every United States senator to discuss the treaties. Administration officials made 775 appearances across the country and the President himself spent over fifty hours of his time speaking to more than 1,500 opinion

[3] Delivered in the US Senate, February 21, 1978. From the *Congressional Record,* February 21, 1978, p S2103–10.

[4] For biographical notes, see Appendix.

leaders about the treaties. On February 1, he devoted a fireside chat to the treaty provisions, and he made a twenty-six-hour trip on February 17-18 through Rhode Island, Maine, and New Hampshire to mend political fences an answer questions about the proposed treaties (*Newsweek,* February 13, 1978, p 18-20).

On March 16, 1978, the resolution of ratification of the first treaty passed the Senate by a vote of 68 to 32. On April 18, the second one was supported by an identical vote (one more than the necessary two-thirds majority). During the long struggle for ratification, wavering senators shifted back and forth from "parochial politics to statesmanship" (Don Farmer, ABC News, April 15, 1978), not revealing their stands until they cast their votes. One source thought that "the eight weeks of actual debate (with two weeks off for vacation) could be easily edited into three or four days of thoughtful comment on broader issues" (Adam Clymer, New York *Times,* April 16, 1978).

The speeches reproduced here were delivered in the Senate on February 21, 1978, during the debate over ratification of the first treaty. Senators Samuel I. Hayakawa (Republican, California) and Daniel P. Moynihan (Democrat, New York) supported ratification and Senator Orrin G. Hatch (Republican, Utah) advocated rejection. The speeches are thoughtful statements by three serious and concerned legislators.

This exchange of arguments had some novel aspects. Hayakawa and Moynihan, both Ph.D.s and former college professors, represented states directly concerned with ocean traffic and use of the canal. Hatch of Utah, like many other opponents, represented an inland state. Richard L. Strout observed that the division between the two sides went "deeper than the normal Democratic-Republican division" and perhaps foreshadowed "American post-Viet attitude toward world affairs" (*Christian Science Monitor,* January 6, 1978). In some ways the debate was reminiscent of the Senate deliberations on the League of Nations fifty-eight years earlier.

Mr. President, as I look back at the early stages of the public debate on the Panama treaties, it seems to me that I was among the first public figures who became actively involved in this issue. My remark, "We stole it fair and square —we should keep it," was good for a laugh and it made headlines. It was a witticism and generally understood as such. During the campaign it was, of course, not possible to go into the subject in depth. But I always made it clear that our policies toward Panama had to be examined in the general framework of our relations with the other countries of Latin America, as the distinguished Senator from South Carolina made so clear.

All through 1977, I have given a great deal of thought to the subject. My final conclusion was that I should vote for the treaties provided certain minimum requirements were met. They were enumerated in my testimony before the Subcommittee on Separation of Powers. In a few minutes, I will discuss the treaties in the light of my four conditions. However, before doing so, I think I should explain why, in principle, I decided in favor of ratification.

As I see it, the issue of ratification involves three considerations: First, the prevailing political and psychological climate: second, moral principles, and third, practical consequences.

As to the first consideration, I have to go back to the historical events of 1903 when Panama became an independent state. You will recall that prior to that date, there had been several abortive attempts by Panamanian nationalists to secede from Colombia. The 1903 revolution succeeded only because of the carefully timed arrival of American naval forces, who prevented Colombian troops from suppressing the uprising.

In some of our contemparary textbooks, this unilateral US action and the subsequent treaty negotiations are usually condemned as an example of despicable imperialism. I object to this evaluation.

What the United States did in 1903 was nothing unusual or contrary to the public mores of those days. At the turn of the century, all great powers behaved similarly, and the speed with which the new Republic was recognized by all the Latin American governments, with the sole exception of Colombia, indicates that we simply acted in accordance with the "Zeitgeist," a term which Webster identifies as the spirit of the age.

Mr. President, I think everybody in this chamber will agree that the spirit of 1977 is very different from the one which prevailed when we signed the treaty with Monsieur Bunau-Varilla, a Frenchman and an early big-time operator. Today, a very different spirit prevails, and it was the United States, which, in its foreign and domestic policies, did its level best to bring the changes about.

That change of climate is our own doing. This, of course, brings me to my second consideration, namely, the aspect of moral principles.

Mr. President, when the British departure from India came under discussion, it was the United States which was in the forefront of those who pressured for full independence. When the end of Dutch control of Indonesia was being negotiated, it was again the United States which suspended aid to the Netherlands East Indies, and followed this up with threats to cut off assistance to the Netherlands as well. Both steps were taken in order to coerce the Dutch Government into a more conciliatory attitude toward Indonesian nationalists.

The liquidation of the French and Belgian Empires in Africa was encouraged by American public opinion and the government of the United States. Moreover, the new political climate was dramatically demonstrated by this country when it intervened in the Suez crisis. It was the United States which prevented the recapture of the Suez Canal by the British Army. It should be recalled that the American Secretary of the Treasury, George Humphrey, at that time gave the British Government a virtual ultimatum. Great Britain was given the simple choice of an immediate cease-fire or war on the pound. Not a dollar would be available for oil supplies. Unless the British advance toward the canal was promptly stopped, the United States would block access to dollars from the International Monetary Fund. It would block credit from the Export-Import Bank, and it would make no effort to aline American bankers behind the pound. If the British persisted in trying to take back the Suez Canal, they would face a forced devaluation and gas rationing. Reluctantly, the British capitulated.

Mr. President, I have cited these excerpts from recent world history to remind this body of the crucial role the United States has played in promoting a new international morality. And I have to ask my colleagues today how could this country possibly have the effrontery to refuse to draw the consequences of its own actions? In the light of recent history, could there by anything more hypocritical than an insistence on the status quo in the Panama Canal.

Let me quote a paragraph or two from the columnist, Vermont Royster, in *The Wall Street Journal.* He served in the Panama Canal Zone in the earlier years of the Second World War. He says:

> There we Americans, civilian and military, had our own housing, our own swimming pools, tennis courts, movie theaters and shops. The cost of all these things was nominal since they were tax-free and subsidized, which was very nice for a young man on an ensign's pay.
>
> Things weren't quite so pleasant for a Panamanian. All these amenities were off-limits to the Panamanians, many of whom lived in near poverty. If a Panamanian did work for the Canal, he got lower wages than his American counterpart and had none of the privileges. He was also constantly reminded of his lower status by such things as separate toilets and separate drinking fountains, marked "gold" for Americans, "silver" for Panamanians.
>
> So I have no trouble understanding the long years of resentment of the Panamanians at their second-class status in their own country and their years of agitation to get the status of the Canal changed.

Or, as Charles McCabe pointed out in the San Francisco *Chronicle* recently:

> The Vietnam adventure also gave us some knowledge of how much the United States is truly disliked in much of the civilized world. In Panama, as an instance, this dislike is almost a part of the atmosphere of the Canal Zone.

My third consideration when reflecting on the issue, namely the practical consequences of rejection, can be quickly summarized. As I see it, rejection would impair all the good will we have in Latin America; it would poison our relations with most of the countries in the Western Hemisphere; it would give new force to the dangerous imagery of Yankee imperialism.

Mr. President, I shall turn now to the treaties which are before the Senate, and examine whether they satisfy the four conditions which I mentioned before. In my testimony, I stated the following:

(1) I would find it unacceptable if the executive branch through its actions preempted the issue and Congress could only rubberstamp a fait accompli.

(2) I would find equally unacceptable any agreements which would lead to the inefficient operation of the Canal and the imposition of an undue burden on American and world commerce by the operators of the Canal.

(3) I would find unacceptable any sudden and drastic changes of present operational and administrative procedures instead of a gradually evolving process.

(4) Finally, I would find it unacceptable if the executive branch negotiated an agreement which would not fully retain control of the military defense of the Canal and enable us to act promptly whenever there appears any challenge to such control.

Taking these up one by one, first, it is clear now that the Congress is not expected any longer to rubberstamp a fait accompli. The Byrd-Baker amendment which was prepared in close cooperation with the administration demonstrates that the objections of the Senate were heard. The effort to include the Senate in these historical deliberations came late—but it did not come too late.

Mr. MOYNIHAN. Will the senator yield?

Mr. HAYAKAWA. I am glad to yield.

Mr. MOYNIHAN. It is with great hesitation that I interrupt a superbly organized and brilliantly succinct presentation. Although this is not the reason for which I rise, I should like to say to my dear friend and distinguished Senator that his recalling of the events at Suez was brilliant.

In 1956, this country would not accept the imperial powers of France and Britain returning to seize by force the Suez Canal, as they had planned to do. George Humphrey—not a man noted for visionary views, scarcely a member of the center of his own party, much less of the world in which it is my pleasure to live politically—George Humphrey knew you could not do that in 1956.

George Humphrey—of the M. A. Hanna Co., the very same Mark Hanna who helped put together the Panama Canal. George Humphrey—fundamentalist, Cleveland capitalist, banker, Republican Cabinet Member, Secretary of the Treasury, in 1956 in effect said to the British and French, "You can't do that, that day is over."

But I would like to congratulate the senator for bringing up that issue, which [will] be heard again in this chamber.

But he asked about the proposal by the majority and minority leaders to amend the treaty to incorporate the statement of President Carter and General Torrijos. It happened that I was in Panama at the time with nine colleagues, a group led by Senators Cranston and Stafford, at the time this question arose.

We met with General Torrijos and his cabinet officers on these matters and we said, "Now, what would be the case if we amended the treaty to incorporate this language? Will that not require a new plebiscite in Panama according to your constitutional provisions with respect to the treaty?"

They were emphatic. They thought carefully. They took twenty-four hours to answer it. Their answer, when it came after a period of time, was the same as their initial response, "No, it will not." Because the general said, and his cabinet agreed, and there is no question of the fact, that the plebiscite took place after the Carter-Torrijos agreements was reached and was made public in Panama. The general went on TV in Panama to say in effect, "Now, when you decide to vote on this plebiscite, remember that the treaty comprehends the agreement, the agreement is simply an expression of our understanding of the treaty."

On this point, the Panamanians are quite clear as to

their own constitutional procedures. I believe it is the case, I understand it to be the case in international law, that one looks to the procedures established by a nation to determine whether or not they have been followed. So I believe I can express to my colleague the feeling, the firm conviction, that no subsequent plebiscite will be needed. The treaty, as we have proposed to vote for it, has already been ratified by Panama.

Mr. HAYAKAWA. I thank the senator from New York, my very good friend, for clarifying this issue.

* * *

The PRESIDING OFFICER (Mr. CLARK): The Chair recognizes the distinguished Senator from Utah.

Mr. HATCH: Mr. President, I want to compliment the distinguished senator from California for many of his ideas.

I would like to take a few minutes, however, at this point in the debate to mention a few things that I think are quite important.

I particularly enjoyed the interesting, if not volatile, recitation of the distinguished senator from South Carolina of some of the military interpretations that he has and his sterling defense of the present members of the Joint Chiefs of Staff. On the other hand, I have to be very concerned that the American people understand that there are, as I understand it, well over three hundred, as many as three hundred and seventy-nine retired generals and admirals who are totally against these treaties because they have read them and they have studied them. They understand the military and security implications of these treaties as well as the present leaders of the Joint Chiefs of Staff.

I do not think anybody really should impugn the members of the Joint Chiefs of Staff because I believe they believe what they have said. As a matter of fact, some of the things that most of them have said before the Senate Armed Services Committee come down to basically,

We wish we could stay in Panama, we wish we could keep the status quo, we wish we could maintain our seventeen or more military bases and air force bases down there, our refueling facilities, and all of the other things that mean so much to the defense of this country and to the security of all of this hemisphere.

But in this imperfect world some of them have said, I think, in those terms, this is about the best we can do. Their understanding is based upon information given to them from, I understand, the State Department, the ambassadors, the administration, and others, and they have accepted these statements.

But I would like to call to the attention of the American people, Mr. President, and of course all of my distinguished colleagues here that four former chiefs of naval operation, Admirals Carey, Anderson, Burke, and Admiral Moorer have all come out strongly opposed to these treaties.

Admiral Moorer is very significant because he was, as I think everybody knows, the chairman of the Joint Chiefs of Staff prior to General Brown, from 1970 to 1974. He has made a number of eloquent statements before various Senate and House committees in this matter, and I think has laid bare many of the weaknesses and erroneous assumptions about these particular treaties.

On the Panama Canal's importance to the US defense interest, Admiral Moorer stated:

> There is no feasible war plan for the United States, taking into account our reduced forces and extended commitments, that does not assume that the Panama Canal will be available for full-time priority use. The only alternative that would permit the meeting of time scales of current war plans based on the threat in both the Atlantic and Pacific Oceans would be a major buildup of naval combat forces overall, together with a very large expansion of supply and communications storage facilities for both the Army and Air Force on both coasts. The utility of the canal has been demonstrated over and over again in times of emergency. World War I, World War II, the Korean War, the Cuba crisis, and the Vietnam war all placed heavy loads on the Panama Canal which were efficiently handled to the great benefit of the United States and her

allies. I see no change whatever in the critical contribution of the canal to our military strength in the near future or in the out years far beyond the meaningless year of 2000.

Admiral Moorer was of the opinion that if the "Canal operation was slowed down or stopped, the timing of any war plan we have immediately collapses." In fact, that is a direct quote from Admiral Moorer.

Concerning the importance of US presence in Panama, Admiral Thomas Moorer stated:

> I believe a permanent US presence in the Panama Canal Zone to be the only feasible and safe posture for all of the nations of this hemisphere.

He then added:

> Do not be surprised if the treaty is ratified in its present form, to see a Soviet and/or Cuban presence quickly established in Panama. In any event, any confrontation over the neutrality of the canal then becomes a confrontation with the Soviet Union rather than with Panamanian guerrillas or terrorists.

In response to the question on the importance of the United States having base rights in Panama after the year 2000, Admiral Moorer responded:

> I think it is mandatory that we maintain a presence through one kind of agreement or another.

With regard to global implications of the treaties, Admiral Moorer stated that:

> The defense and use of the Panama Canal is wrapped inextricably with the overall global strategy of the United States and the security of the free world.
>
> I submit that, if the United States opts to turn over full responsibility for the maintenance and operations of such an important waterway to a very small, resource poor and unstable country as Panama and then withdraws all US presence, a vacuum will be created which will quickly be filled by proxy or directly by the Soviet Union as is their practice at every opportunity.

The admiral also noted that:

> Anyone who has observed Soviet actions since World War II and studied their literature concerning maritime affairs soon learns that the Soviets fully understand the importance of the Panama Canal.

He added that:

> The prime reason that the Soviet Union accepts the burdensome support of Cuba is due to their desire to dominate the Caribbean, including the Panama Canal, as they greatly expand their maritime capabilities—both warship and merchant ships. We have here the development of a Torrijos-Castro-Moscow Axis.

He brought out some pretty important things on the internal threat to the canal on a variety of occasions, but let me skip that for now and talk about some of his comments concerning Panama's ability to operate and defend the canal.

Concerning Panama's capability to run the canal, Admiral Moorer stated:

> The overall capability of Panama to maintain and operate the canal after the year 2000 when the United States is required to withdraw is a troublesome point.

He further noted that "the Panama Canal with its locks, pumps, and electrical controls is extremely more complex technically than the sea-level Suez Canal. Furthermore, Panama is a very small country with a population about the size of Atlanta, Ga., that is, 1.7 million. She is led by a military dictator with Marxist leanings," Admiral Moorer says. In fact he goes on to say, "political opponents have been exiled. Until recently all political activity has been outlawed. The press is controlled. The country is heavily in debt, and spending forty percent of its income carrying its debt. Panama has no heavy industry worth the name and is woefully lacking in management skills as evidenced by the fact that several large-scale construction projects attempted recently have failed. It is very doubtful whether Panama will acquire the capability to maintain and efficiently operate an industrial complex the size of the Panama Canal, even long after the year 2000."

On Panama's ability to defend the canal, the Admiral stated:

> One must consider the contribution of the Panamanian Armed Forces in the defense of the canal. What will happen when the United States leaves in the year 2000 under the terms of these proposed treaties? How long before the canal falls in unfriendly hands? With the second smallest population in Latin America, Panama's army consists of nothing more than 1,500 light infantry with no modern equipment. In addition, there are about 6,000 of the Guardia Nacional who are assigned police duties, including making certain that Torrijos remains in power through removal of political opponents. It is apparent that some of the Guardia Nacional, such as Colonel Noriega, the Director of Intelligence, are hostile to the United States . . . . In any event, Panama's capability to defend the canal is practically nil.

William P. Clements, Jr., former Deputy Secretary of Defense, testified in opposition to the treaties. He stated the treaties "were far too complex," deploring the "multiplicity of instruments" and the "ambiguous" clauses. He favored a "complete overhaul" of the treaties and focused his opposition on three points—defense, economic considerations, and US rights to build a new sea-level canal.

With regard to defense aspects, Secretary Clements found the security clause of the treaties "totally unacceptable." He revealed that in 1975 at the request of President Ford he went to Panama with Joint Chiefs' Chairman George Brown and negotiated with General Torrijos a security clause which was later agreed to by all US parties, including the State Department and the National Security Council. Secretary Clements testified that Torrijos also approved this clause and it "was included in the then existing draft of the treaty" and remained intact "in the treaty as proposed until sometime after January 20, 1977." The agreement, as reported by Secretary Clements and printed in the committee record, was as follows:

In the event of any threat to the neutrality or security of the canal, the Parties shall consult concerning joint and individual efforts, to secure respect for the canal's neutrality and security through diplomacy, conciliation, mediation, arbitration, the International Court of Justice, or other peaceful means. If such efforts would be inadequate or have proved to be inadequate, each party shall take such other diplomatic, economic or military measures as it deems necessary in accordance with its constitutional process.

In other words, what Secretary Clements was saying is that they had worked out a neutrality agreement that better protected American security, that was agreed to by the Panamanians in 1975, and written into the body of the earlier treaty. This original language is far superior to what we have in these treaties today, because it would have given the United States greater protection, and would have solved some of the problems of international law which have been raised here.

That is very important, and it amazes me that our present ambassadors are trying to sell us a clause that does not come close to the guarantees of the original language.

First they try to sell us an ambiguous treaty without adequate neutrality provisions protecting the United States in any way. They argued that if we ever changed the treaties, my goodness gracious, Panama would have to have a new plebiscite. They even disagreed with my distinguished friend the senator from New York (Mr. Moynihan) that international law would take [care] of the problem.

So President Carter and Mr. Torrijos got together and orally agreed on this new statement of principle, which is not one-fifth as effective, as impressive, as legal, or as clear and straightforward under international law as what had formerly been agreed to by both sides. All we have to do is agree to this wonderful new oral agreement, which they reduced to an unsigned document, which I would submit is not worth the paper that it was not signed on. And that if we would do that, there would not have to be a plebiscite.

Now, as a result of some of the forceful arguments that

many of us have made all over this country, and the fears and concerns of the American people, the distinguished majority leader and the distinguished minority leader, have come forth with an amendment supported by seventy-seven cosponsors and are going to try to amend the treaties now, something they said could not be done without a plebiscite. Or at least that is my understanding of it. Now they are willing to amend the treaties, and I understand the distinguished senior senator from New York, my dear friend Mr. Javits, has said these amendments will not add anything to the prior treaty, that everything was implied in the prior treaty; but I understand he also is a cosponsor of these amendments.

What I am saying is this: To ignore better than three hundred generals and admirals who have served this country patriotically and with distinction in favor of these supportive-to-the-administration statements of our present chairman of the Joint Chiefs of Staff and other members of the Joint Chiefs, is tragic, and I think it is detrimental to this country—especially Admiral Moorer, who was recently chairman of the Joint Chiefs of Staff, and incidentally knows every aspect of the canal. I do not mean to denigrate the Army or Air Force, but I have to admit the Navy really understands the operational aspects and importance of the canal, I think, much better than any other branch.

To ignore the other three former chiefs of naval operations is equally tragic. To accept what the State Department has to say at face value, after all the appeasement we have gone through in the last thirty or forty years, while this country has gone downhill in the eyes of almost everyone in the world, would be a serious error.

I do not want to reflect on the present Joint Chiefs, because I believe them all to be honorable men and good men. But I do think that they should have looked at the many years of appeasement that we have gone through, the many years of mistakes by the State Department—mistakes prophesied by many Senators who sit in this sacred body.

Secretary Clements testified that lawyers in the Defense and State Departments assured him the words in this clause, "as it deems necessary," gave the United States the "unilateral right" to intervene to assure the security of the canal.

Secretary Clements found the new clause—and remember, Secretary Clements is the former Deputy Secretary of Defense—he found the new clause, relating to the maintenance of the "regime of neutrality" "ambiguous" and expressed the opinion that if Torrijos agreed to the clause he had negotiated in 1975 then stronger words than those in the present treaties are and should be negotiable.

Secretary Clements also testified that in his opinion and that of international lawyers with whom he had talked neither article IV nor the Torrijos-Carter understanding gave the United States a clear right to intervene.

I would just mention for the record that what we are doing here is a very serious matter. I would like to join in supporting my good friend, the distinguished senator from Alabama (Mr. Allen), who, in my opinion, is one of the greatest senators sitting in the US Senate, certainly one of the leading parliamentarians in the Senate, and perhaps the constitutional authority in the Senate. I would like to support him where he indicated that he hopes, and I hope likewise, that our distinguished colleagues in the Senate do not get so bound up in partisan support of the administration's desires that we abdicate our responsibility, or, should I say, responsibilities, to see that these treaties, if they have to be ratified in the end, or if we have to advise and consent to them, at least are protective of the United States of America; that they take our needs into consideration; that these treaties resolve these ambiguous problems; that they resolve the translation problems so that there is no question in the minds of our friends, the Panamanians, or any questions in our minds, as to the effect, legal or otherwise, of these treaties.

I think some pretty effective and important amendments are about to come forth on this floor. I have some amend-mends which I think are monumentally important, and which I hope my colleagues will consider in helping to make these treaties much better than they are right now.

I have made the comment that a second-year law student in one of the major institutions, and I do not mean a mental institution but a law institution, can do a better job writing these treaties than what has been done.

I cite the statement of Secretary Clements, who did an adequate job, if not the best job, with regard to the neutrality language that they had worked out with Mr. Torrijos earlier.

I believe it is important for us to realize that it is wonderful to have friendships and relationships with Panama. I do not think anything is really going to change that, because most of us want to continue a good, cordial relationship with our Panamanian neighbors. This has come about through years and years of working with them and years and years of experience with Panama. I think most of us love the Panamanian people. I do not think they would expect us to not protect the United States of America, since that is our primary job as US Senators.

If these treaties, which I find to be reprehensible, poorly written, legally unsound, filled with ambiguities, filled with construction difficulties between the English and Spanish translations, are not corrected, then I have to admit I would not blame any citizen or the millions of citizens of this country if they hold it against us the rest of their lives.

The proposals should bring about some changes, which, in my opinion, are long overdue anyway, because of the last forty or forty-one years of control by one philosophy of the Congress, particularly in the Senate.

I think the people of this country, and I regret to say this but I think it is true, have inherited, the vast majority of them, more knowledge about these treaties than any of my protreaty colleagues have been willing to admit.

I think in spite of the polls, which still show that most of our people are overwhelmingly against these treaties, if the truth were really known seventy-five to eighty percent of the people in this country will not buy these treaties.

I think it is pretty important that we, as US Senators, give every consideration to all amendments which will be proposed, especially those which tend to make these treaties more understandable, and especially those amendments which would tend to protect the Constitution.

Concerning our colleagues in the other House of this coequal branch of government, and especially those amendments which pertain to solving the ambiguities of the treaties, especially those amendments which pertain to clarifying the need to have all appropriations bills originate in the House, in advance, rather than bringing them back after a fait accompli has been accomplished, I think if we ignore them, as the distinguished majority leader has said he is going to do—and I assume with his leadership majority are going to follow in a partisan way—if we ignore the House of Representatives in this matter, then I cannot blame them later if they refuse to grant anything that any administration would want with regard to the problems that are bound to arise as a result of our failure to do our job legally, internationally, and otherwise to resolve the problems of these treaties.

It is discouraging to me that there seems to be such a lack of understanding, a sense of uncertainty. There are certain protreaty members who have made a great study of this matter, of course, of all matters involved here. Unfortunately, I do not believe that the majority of those who will vote for these treaties have really done everything they can to try to protect American interests.

I believe this is a pretty serious matter. I consider the Panama Canal treaties one of the most important issues to come before the Congress. I think there will be few other major important issues. Of course, what we do with agriculture, energy, and labor reform, are of significance. What we do on SALT II is even more important.

I believe this year is going to determine whether the

United States of America continues to be the leader of the world, the leader of freedom in the world, the country to which the other nations point toward freedom and look up to.

I think if these treaties have to be ratified—and I have not given in to the belief that 67 senators in the Senate are going to vote their consent to the ratification—I happen to believe that if they are going to be ratified my colleagues should be concerned about having ratified treaties which are worth while, which have unambiguous meanings for solving some of these very great problems which are being raised. If we have the treaties, let them be right.

I can say this: I have always been, from the beginning of the debate in this matter, in favor of reviewing the 1903 Treaty.

I have always been for treating our Panamanian neighbors well and decently. I think there are many ways we could do that without these treaties. I still think there are many ways that we could have a cordial and decent relationship with Panama and still have the indiscriminate, inexpensive and, I think, expeditious management of the canal which the United States has rendered for so many years, for the benefit of everybody in the world, not just us. I think many people are concerned about these treaties. I think our obligation is, if we have to have ratification, to make sure that we are not ratifying a pig in a poke. I suspect that if these treaties are ratified with only the amendments of our distinguished colleagues, the majority and minority leaders, then we are going to have troubles the rest of our lives that far transcend even some of the troubles that are being raised if these treaties are not ratified.

On the other hand, if we could have enough amendments to clarify and make these treaties the effective treaties they should be, beneficial to the United States, taking into consideration our needs as well as our Panamanian neighbors' and friends' needs, then I think there would be a great deal less hostility engendered in this country toward those who vote for the treaties and those who do so without very good consideration of the needs of our country, in the rapt desire to satisfy and pacify the Panamanian dictator and others, who I do not really believe are friends of the United States of America.

As a matter of fact, I do not think these treaties are going to create any friendship toward the United States of America. I think if anything showed up as the result of the private hearings, the secret hearings, on the drug issue, the thing that did show up is that we have some pretty sleazy people down there with which we are going to have to deal for many, many years, and that their interests are certainly not going to be those of the United States. Nor are they going to coincide with regularity with those of the United States of America.

So, I appeal to my distinguished colleagues to consider every good, substantive amendment to these treaties and maybe, in the process, there will be some support for the treaties that would otherwise never be expected. Maybe, in the process, we shall save ourselves untold embarrassment, difficulties, and entanglements which could hurt this country and many, many other free countries and people who rely on the United States to have some guts in this world and to stand up for its rights once in a while.

I think that there are many things on both sides of this issue that anybody can be for. I think there are good arguments on both sides. My personal belief is that, unless these treaties are seriously and significantly amended and modified to protect this country and to protect our interests, no reasonable senator should vote and give his consent to the ratification of these treaties. Although this is not the time to get into a debate on the constitutional issue, and I shall not do that at this time, I believe that any senator who fails to recognize the importance of 219 members of the House of Representatives, some of whom are for these treaties, and their right to approve the transfer of ten billion dollars of American properties—at least five different types of American property—is, I think, allowing an unconstitutional act to occur.

I am going to bring up an amendment which will get into that detail, and I am sure we can debate it at that time. But I think that my colleagues should consider, and consider well, just how important these treaties are, reject the partisan approaches that I sense on the floor of the Senate, and start working to have these treaties properly corrected. This is our duty, our solemn obligation, and our right. I think if we will, we shall have done the Senate a great service. We shall have added to the prestige of, and respect for, the Senate. We shall have done the President a great service, because he is much less likely to suffer in the future in the eyes of the historians. And I think that it would create a lot of good will and good feeling all over this country among our American citizens and constituents, whom we all represent.

I might just add—does the distinguished senator from New York wish me to yield?

Mr. Moynihan: I rise to take the opportunity to state that I had hoped the senator would speak longer. I have listened with great absorption to all the things he has said. My point cannot be made as a parliamentarian. I shall listen with further patience and sure addition to my meager stock of knowledge.

Mr. Hatch: I appreciate the statement of the distinguished senator from New York. I do have some other things I wish to say, but I can see that he might have some points to make, so I yield at this time.

Mr. Moynihan: I thank the senator from Utah for his graciousness and for his learned, careful ways. He would know that there could have been few persons to come into the chamber in recent years with as pronounced a sense of fairness and a concern about accuracy and a civility of manner. It was typically courteous of him to allow me to speak at this point. To begin, may I say what is not always easy to say, and not always the most useful thing to raise, in this chamber. I have been struck by the pattern of the vote taken yesterday, an important vote, Mr. President, a vote in which it became clear that these treaties, products really of the past four Presidents, will be ratified. The Senate of the United States will advise and consent to their ratification. The vote yesterday clearly marked the moment in which the Senate was first on record as favoring these treaties.

What struck me was the geographical disparity as between those who voted to support the treaties and those who could not yet do so.

There are twenty-three American states which border on the high seas, whose shores are touched with saltwater, whose lives are much involved with navigation and commerce on the high seas.

I was struck how senators from these states were so overwhelmingly in favor of these treaties; indeed my state of New York is nothing if not a commercial seagoing, outward bound state. I see that the junior senator from Maryland is on the floor. I note that the senators representing Baltimore, the senators who represent San Francisco, Oakland, Seattle, and up and down and around the coast support these treaties. Altogether there were only ten senators, only ten senators of the forty-six which represent the twenty-three seagoing states, who voted against these treaties.

Of those who did, overwhelmingly they were from another bloc of states that voted "no," which is from the state of the old South. Thus, two groups of senators voted "no." Those from the high plains and those from the old South.

Since I have the respect which we all have for all of these senators, it seemed to me to confirm a thought that has been in my mind, which is that there are not ten members of this body who truly do not support these treaties. But there are a number of those who are legitimately concerned that the people in their own states do not.

It is the high plains and the Old South that find these

treaties worrisome, that find the subject unfamiliar and threatening, and somehow fear that we will lose what we must hold onto if we approve the treaties.

These are proper and honorable concerns. I would wish to speak to them. I should wish to speak first to a point which is, perhaps, difficult to make, but it is necessary: That the times have changed, the world has changed, and for all the glory that the Panama Canal represented, for all the extraordinary ability that it stands, for the incomparable, palpable manifestation of American achievement that it is, that it should somehow end in fear and alarm in a world of separate drinking fountains, one gold, the other silver, separating people.

When I was in Panama in a delegation led by Senator Cranston and Senator Stafford, it happened that that day in the Miami *Herald,* a lieutenant commander, retired, US Navy, wrote to the paper a letter which was published that day describing the events in 1964 when a riot occurred in the zone, and between the zone and Panama, when persons were killed, when President Johnson reacted to an emergency he had not expected, when the present sequence of negotiations began, involving four Presidents and culminating in this debate on the treaty. This US naval commander —I noted that he was US Navy, and he was not a Reserve commander, he was obviously a regular naval officer—described how painful it was to see, in which, a group of young Panamanian students who in accordance with the prior agreement came forward bearing a Panamanian flag which they were going to raise on the flagpole as agreed. Young Americans, egged on, as this letter said, by adults cheering and jeering at them, proceeded to beat up the Panamanians, to discredit their flag, to do the most awful things, things which we associate with the worst, the least agreeable and dishonorable aspects of a frightened colonialist mentality. How inappropriate to this Republic, how rare in our experience, and how squalid an episode in the aftermath of the glory of this canal.

Now, this is the point: We are not retreating by this move; we are advancing. If we advise and consent to the ratification of these treaties, we will see a transformation of the world scene as we have not seen in a generation.

At long last, the charge and the curse and the burden of imperialism, the greatest democracies of Europe, and the less consequential, but similar and real charge against the United States, will have been put into the past honorably, with courage, manfully. And what will remain in the world but the one last nineteenth century empire, not only undiminished in the twentieth century, but expanded? The empire of the czars and the new czars, astride the Continent from the Pacific to the Atlantic, to the Bosporus, now into the Red Sea, now into the Indian Ocean, now into the South Atlantic, with its Gurkhas from Havana, its Afrika Korps recruited to do the murdering and burning and killing. The Soviet empire, finally, will emerge as what it is, an abomination, an anachronism, a threat to the peace of the world against which the best loving and best needing nations of the world must combine.

Far from a retreat, ratification of these treaties will turn the world on its heel. The United States can go forward as it has not done since the great days of the second world war when we stood almost alone in the defense of freedom.

The distinguished senator from Utah speaks of this year as one in which it will be judged whether the United States remains a leader of freedom in the world. It will be, and it will be determined by whether or not we ratify these treaties.

I think it so important and I was so pleased by the statement, the reference of the distinguished junior senator from California, who reminded us that there was a reality in the way we obtained the canal. It was not attractive, but it was characteristic of the time.

But we have ever since been the anti-imperialist, anti-colonialist force in the world.

We are the nation that stated to the British they must

get out of India. It was Franklin D. Roosevelt who started saying that to an unbelieving Churchill in 1943. It was the United States that said to the Dutch that they must leave Indonesia. We said to the French that they had no help in Algeria. We said the same thing to Spain and to Portugal. Incidentally, remember, in 1935, the United States said it would have an end to colonial rule in the Philippines. It happened that came in 1945 on schedule, in 10 years' time. . . .

Those who have read the extraordinary and careful report of the Committee on Foreign Relations of the US Senate, of which the senator from Idaho is the second-ranking member, and will soon be the chairman, will note that on page 47 there is a short description of the not perhaps widely known but important fact that the canal probably would have been built in Nicaragua had it not been for the energy of Mr. Bunau-Varilla and a particularly active New York lawyer named William Nelson Cromwell, of the firm of Sullivan and Cromwell. Mr. Cromwell had the great coup of enlisting the support of Senator Mark Hanna of Ohio, who had helped elect President McKinley—previously Senator McKinley—and was a great force—and had been appointed to the Senate—and a great influence on this nation; not perhaps a progressive one with respect to some social policies but certainly a forward-looking one with respect to the structure of the American economy. That was in 1903.

A mere fifty-three years passed, and the British and the French invaded the Suez with armies. The distinguished senator spoke of our having preached against colonialism. Certainly, we spoke of it as a moral issue, and the word "preach" is altogether appropriate. We did more than preach. We acted.

In that October 1956, the Secretary of the Treasury said to the British Government:

> If you persist, we will break the pound. You will have food rationing and unemployment and depression as you have never

known. We will break the pound with the power of the dollar, because there is an issue of principle here.

Who was this man, the Secretary of the Treasury? He was Mr. George Humphrey: And what had he done in his life? In 1918, he had joined the M. A. Hanna Co. of Cleveland and had risen to be its president in 1952, when he joined the Eisenhower Cabinet. Was George Humphrey a radical? Was he a visionary? Was he a man given to soft and unsuspecting views of the world? No. Alas, no, he was not.

Did he think that the whole weight of American power should be put against the effort of the British and the French to regain control of the Suez? Yes; he did, because he knew in 1956—the president of the M. A. Hanna Co. knew in 1956—that you cannot do things like that any more. Yet, here we are in 1978 wondering whether what we absolutely forbade the British and French to do, we should somehow insist upon for ourselves.

I should like to speak to the extraordinary success of our negotiations and the fact that we have learned something from this history, unlike the French, driven out of their possessions, and the British, in effect driven out of their position in the canal, going back in that squalid and doomed enterprise. Compare the dignity, the manfulness with which we leave—a measure of dignity, while retaining the full measure of our rights and responsibilities. One of the extraordinary and ominous facts of the world was the degree not five years ago to which the Panama Canal issue had been transformed from a bilateral problem between Panama and the United States into an international problem. Panama is not a major strategic issue in the world. It is not an area of any overriding geopolitical concern to the large powers. The nations that depend upon it for commerce are the liberal nations of northern South America, I think we can basically say. It has not engaged the military or economic concerns of the world.

However, in the beginning of the 1970's, it became a

great symbolic issue, an issue of the ideological clash between North and South, between liberal societies and the totalitarian societies which would side with the South, and it was an issue on which we were hopelessly outnumbered, completely misunderstood, and at least partially in the wrong, by our own standards.

This perhaps will not any longer remain a secret. I hope I am not subject to censure for recalling that in our closed session the other day I raised the question of the meeting of the Security Council of the United Nations which took place in Panama City in March of 1973. I think it would be useful to go back to that not distant time, five years ago, and to recall the atmosphere and the events of that moment.

In 1972, for the first time, the Security Council met outside of New York, met in Addis Ababa, and shortly thereafter, the Panamanian government proposed that the next meeting be in Panama City. For a moment, it looked as though there was a move to take the Security Council away from its headquarters in New York altogether and have it move around to colonial areas of the world where, as the General Assembly had already become, it would become a forum in which the judges sitting with the verdicts in their pockets would hear the indictment of the United States and of the liberal democracies still left in the world.

Sure enough, the meeting began in the spring, in March of 1973, and representatives of forty nations spoke before the Security Council. One by one, as President Ford stated in his 1974 message to Congress reporting on the activities of the United States in the U.N. for the previous year, a majority of the independent nations of Latin America, and indeed a third of the membership of the U.N., rose to demand, one after the other—and I quote President Ford's message:

> Most of these supported the Panamanian position that the 1903 US-Panama Isthmian Canal Convention should be abrogated and Panama should be given effective sovereignty over the Panama Canal.

A draft resolution was voted on at the end of the meeting, on March 21, a resolution, cosponsored—and I shall give some of the cosponsors: Guinea, Peru, Sudan, Yugoslavia, tyrannical states, arrayed in their hostility to the United States, except when it comes time for the United States to give them military aid, as in the case of Yugoslavia, which by the way then becomes temporarily more sweet.

In the end, the Security Council voted 13 to 1 against the United States, to condemn the United States, to disassociate itself from the United States. Our friends on the Council, and there were some like Britain, France, they also voted against us. We had to resort to the veto to save ourselves from the formal condemnation of the Security Council.

KEEPING THE SENATE INDEPENDENT [5]

THOMAS J. MCINTYRE [6]

The conservatives who opposed the treaties with Panama conducted what Peter C. Stuart called "one of the most massive and costly lobbying campaigns in American history" (*Christian Science Monitor,* March 10, 1978). In efforts to defeat the treaties the Conservative Caucus, a self-styled "new Right" organization, spent $1,015,000 and the American Conservative Union spent $1,040,000. Other antitreaty forces included veterans groups like the American Legion and Veterans of Foreign Wars and research and education oriented conservative organizations such as the American Security Council and the Conservative Victory Fund.

The public lobby on behalf of the treaties was made up of the Committee of Americans for the Canal Treaties and New Directions, a public affairs lobby that was a global counterpart to Common Cause. This lobby receives help from labor unions, church groups, and liberal organizations such as the Americans for Democratic Action. In comparison to $2.3 million spent by the opponents, the proponents spent about $458,000.

The campaign to rally public support was largely a "mailbox war." The two principal conservative lobbies each mailed more than two million letters, while the pro-New Directions sent out slightly over a million pieces. In addition, part of the persuasion included newspaper advertisements, billboards, booklets, and professional lobbying (*Christian Science Monitor,* March 10, 1978).

In the course of the Senate debate over ratification, March 1, 1978, Thomas J. McIntyre (Democrat, New Hampshire) gave a rousing speech concerning the pressures that the conservative groups were bringing upon the senators. Richard L. Strout called it "one of the strongest speeches" that Congress had "heard for some time" (*Christian Science Monitor,* March 10, 1978).

Robert C. Byrd (Democrat, West Virginia), majority leader of the Senate, offered high praise of the speech, saying:

> In my thirty-two years in public office I have not heard many political speeches, many speeches dealing with legisla-

[5] Delivered before the US Senate, March 1, 1978. Title supplied by editor. From the *Congressional Record,* March 1, 1978, p S2592–5.

[6] For biographical note, see Appendix.

> tive matters, many speeches dealing with any matters, for that part, that really move me.
>
> Few speeches in this Chamber change votes.
>
> I wish that all the Members of the Senate had the opportunity to be present to hear the speech that has just been delivered by the distinguished senior Senator from New Hampshire. I class this speech as being among the two or three speeches I have heard in thirty-two years in public office that have had a genuine impact on my thinking, on me personally, and I believe on all who have had the privilege to listen to it.

The speech made an important point about the responsibility of legislators to give the country their best judgments in times of crisis. It also indicated that many senators thought that their individual decisions on ratification were among the most difficult that they had to make in some time.

Mr. President, despite the threats of political reprisal from the radical right, I intend to vote to ratify the proposed Panama Canal treaties.

After six months of hard study, I have concluded that on balance the new treaties are the surest means of keeping the canal open, neutral, and accessible to our use—and are in keeping with our historical commitment to deal fairly and justly with lesser powers.

But no instrument forged by man is perfect and few issues black and white. So I must respect the judgment of those here and in New Hampshire who have given the treaties the same intense and objective scrutiny I have given them, yet—in equally clear conscience—cannot support ratification.

Today, Mr. President, I want to say a few words about how I reached my decision on the treaties. After that, I intend to deliver a full expression of my views on how this issue has been politicized and exploited.

As to the treaties themselves, I promised the people of New Hampshire early last fall that I would neither rush—nor be stampeded—into superficial judgment.

I have kept my word. I made it a point to study the history of the canal, to study the provisions of the original treaty and of the new documents, to consult with those whose judgment I respect, and to ask the hardest questions I could put to those who witnessed for or against ratification in the hearings conducted by the Committee on Armed Services.

I must say that there was never any real question in my mind about the need to modernize our treaty relationship with Panama, Mr. President. That need is as evident to most of us—including many who oppose the new treaties—as it has been to the last four administrations.

Nor did I agonize over the question of sovereignty. As William Buckley put it:

> Even if we had in our hand a record that showed that every Panamanian in 1903 had voted to grant the US in perpetuity the rights we have enjoyed in that area, still there is the shifting perspective between what was permissible and even welcome in 1903, and what is permissible and welcome in 1978.

It was also apparent to me early on that there were considerable risks in rejecting the treaties out of hand because Panama's form of government and negotiating tactics were not precisely to our liking.

It seemed to me that refusing to ratify the treaties for those reasons alone would play into the hands of our adversaries in the Soviet Union and Cuba, would offend most of our neighbors in the Western Hemisphere, might trigger a political upheaval in Panama that would replace the Torrijos regime with one even more fiercely nationalistic and perhaps more repressive, and might cripple our own President's capacity to conduct foreign policy for the remainder of his time in office.

Now I do not like doing business with dictators, either, Mr. President, and particularly with those whose family members may have trafficked in drugs. But, I do not like doing business with dictators of either the left or the right, and I have been struck by the irony that many of those who are in such public high dudgeon over the repression of human rights in Panama ignore or even excuse the same repression of freedom in South Korea, for example, or South Africa.

The hard truth is that there are times when diplomacy, like politics, forces unfastidious bedfellows upon us whether we like it or not. Omar Torrijos is a diplomatic fact of life who at the moment cannot be wished away. But there is consolation in the fact that he will not be around twenty-two years from now when control of the canal finally would pass into Panamanian hands under the terms of the new treaties.

What I am saying, Mr. President, is that I have never believed that offended sensitivities and ruffled chauvinism were sufficient grounds for summarily rejecting the new treaties. We are too big to be that petty.

Instead, I felt that the provisions of the treaties should be measured on their merits by putting them to the test of three crucial questions:

First. Are the new treaties in our best national security interests? Are they, indeed, the best mutually acceptable instruments for insuring the security and the neutrality of the canal, and our ready access to it?

Second. Are the new treaties consistent with the principles upon which our own nation was founded? Do they honor our historical commitment to justice and the right of self-determination for all nations?

Third. Are there any omissions or ambiguities in these treaties that could in time surprise and embitter either signatory and break down the friendship and cooperation they were supposed to enhance?

I sought positive answers and firm assurances from both the Pentagon and the State Department. Mr. President, and some, I must say, were distressingly slow in forthcoming. Indeed, I did not get a definitive response from the State Department regarding what the new treaties would cost us—and give Panama—in dollar terms until late last week, and one point requires still further clarification. Specifically, I am not entirely persuaded that the Panamanian government agrees with our interpretation that any accrued unpaid balance of the annual contingent ten-million-dollar payment will not be paid by the United States. So I am reserving my option to support a clarifying amendment or even an understanding on this point, Mr. President.

In general, however, I am satisfied that both the Pentagon and the State Department have made earnest and honest attempts to provide the answers and the assurances I sought, and to support this judgment I ask unanimous consent that the text of letters of response from Admiral J. L. Holloway, Chief of Naval Operations, regarding security questions, and from the State Department, regarding economic questions, appear in the *Record* at the close of my remarks.

Mr. President, my oath of office required me to make as certain as I could that our security interests would not be jeopardized by the new treaties. Admiral Holloway's testimony before the Committee on Armed Services and his written response to my follow-up questions provided the assurance I sought.

My duty to the taxpayers of this country required me to do all I could to make certain all of the potential dollar costs of the new treaties were fully known and understood. And most of them now are. In some, the American people may have to pay more than they expected, and the Panamanian people may have to settle for less than they anticipated. What is most important, however, is that all of this is known before the final vote on the treaties.

That said, Mr. President, let me now turn to my second purpose here today.

I want to express myself on the way the issue of the canal treaties has been politicized, and I will do so with no little anger and resentment. Perhaps what I am going to say is not precisely germane to the question before us, but I believe with all my heart that it must be said and said now.

The campaign waged by certain opponents of ratification—in my state and across the nation—has impugned the loyalty and the motives of too many honorable Americans to be ignored or suffered in silence a minute longer.

Mr. President, I believe the techniques used to exploit the issue of the canal treaties are the most compelling evidence to date that an ominous change is taking place in the very character and direction of American politics.

In his farewell broadcast several months ago, Eric Sevareid warned of the paradoxical rise of "dangerously passionate certainties" in a time of no easy answers.

One could speculate endlessly about the root cause of this development: A generation of disillusion and disenchantment with the lack of integrity and the misuse of power by leaders and institutions; the humbling experience in Vietnam; the unrelenting pressure of unfocused anxieties about national direction and purpose; and the all-too-human inclination to turn in frustration to the slogans and rostrums of a simpler time.

But whatever the cause, Mr. President, I see abundant evidence that these "dangerously passionate certainties" are being cynically fomented, manipulated, and targeted in ways that threaten amity, unity, and the purposely [sic] course of government in order to advance a radical ideology that is alien to mainstream political thought.

Already we have seen the vigor of the two-party system sapped by this phenomenon. More and more Americans appear unwilling to abide by the essential ethic of the party system—that willingness to tolerate differing views within the party, and to accept the party platform, however unpalatable some of its provisions, in order to advance a general political philosophy.

As a result, the traditional role of the parties is slowly being usurped by a thousand and one passionately committed special interest, splinter faction, and single issue constituencies.

My colleagues know what I am talking about. They

know, as I know, that on any given issue someone somewhere can depress a computer key and within hours or a few days at the most we are inundated by mimeographed post cards and custom-tailored letters and telegrams that vary scarcely a comma in the message they deliver.

Now let me make this clear, Mr. President. I believe in listening to my constituents. I do pay careful heed to all of their cards and letters. But I give special consideration to those that are obviously the individual product of the writer.

And let me say, too, that I believe in firm and outspoken commitment to principles and convictions. I would readily agree, as someone once said, that there are times when compromise offers little more than an "easy refuge for the irresolute spirit."

If the senator from Utah would allow me the opportunity to deliver this talk I would be happy to yield to his questions at the end and, I think, he may have many more questions at the end than he has now.

Mr. HATCH: I would be delighted to delay my questions.

Mr. MCINTYRE: But I would make a distinction between commitment that is rooted in reality—commitment, for example, that recognizes the linkage between problems and the consequences of ignoring that linkage when applying solutions—and commitment that denies reality and is, in truth, but the blind and obsessive pursuit of illusion.

Extremists who deny reality in the pursuit of illusion deny something else, Mr. President, something of fundamental importance in our republic of free men and women. They deny the differences that distinguish one human being from another.

They deny the indisputable fact that each of us is the result of a unique combination of genes and chromosomes, of influences and impressions, of training and of faith, and of the milieu from which we sprang. In short, they deny everything that science and simple observation tell us about human nature and individual capacities and limitations.

By proceeding from the flawed premise that all of us are alike, it is easy for ideologues to conclude that we must see every issue as they see it—unless there is something sinister in our motivation.

And they proceed from that premise, Mr. President, with an arrogance born of the conviction that they and they alone have a corner on patriotism, morality, and God's own truths, that their values and standards and viewpoints are so unassailable they justify any means, however coarse and brutish, of imposing them on others.

Now I want to be fair about this, Mr. President. In the particular instance of the canal treaties, I am talking about the kind of politics practiced by what has come to be known as the New Right. But I want to note that the record of extremists on the ideological left bears a remarkable, and regrettable, similarity.

In his book, *The Education of a Public Man,* Hubert Humphrey said some of his fellow liberals "demanded a purity of performance that is virtually beyond human capability"; that they were happy only when they lost and unhappy when they won because their interest lies only in persuading themselves that they are always in the right.

"There are those," he wrote, "who live by the strict rule that whatever they think is right is necessarily right. They will compromise on nothing. They insist that everyone follow their thinking." And, he added, the wrath of the intellectual liberal at those who are willing to compromise to secure some worthwhile gain is something unbounded.

Hubert Humphrey understood, as Voltaire understood, how frequently "the perfect is the enemy of the good."

There have been times when some of us have felt the wrath of the purist left, Mr. President. And now—today—many of us are feeling the wrath of the New Right because we will not bow to their threats and vote against ratification of the canal treaties.

Indeed, Mr. President, one element of the New Right—

the Conservative Caucus—did not wait for me to announce how I would vote on the treaties. They launched their attack months ago.

Last summer the national director of the Conservative Caucus, Howard Phillips, said conservatives should make "a political sitting duck" of Tom McIntyre over the canal treaties and that the Conservative Caucus could, "make it a political impossibility for McIntyre to vote for that treaty."

On December 4, 1977, the Conservative Caucus of New Hampshire passed a resolution of censure and served it on me like a subpena. I was "censured" for a speech I made last September, a speech in which I took neither side on the treaty issue but merely spelled out the pro and con arguments I would have to consider when I finally made my decision on how to vote.

So that my colleagues can consider the full text and tone of that resolution, I ask unanimous consent to have it appear in the *Record* at the conclusion of my remarks.

The resolution censured me for allegedly giving aid to a recognized dictator, one Omar Torrijos; for indicating I was willing to violate the Constitution and my oath of office by even considering a vote for treaty ratification; for failing to recognize through my speech and "personal ignorance" that the treaties would provide the Communist regimes with a legal beachhead from which they would eventually overpower all nations of Central and South America; for saying in the speech that however I voted I would vote in "good conscience"; for happening to be chairman of the Subcommittee on Financial Institutions when, the resolution said, "it is common knowledge that the financial institutions of the United States have more than a vested interest in the canal treaties."

Not only did the resolution censure me, it required me to appear before the caucus in Wolfeboro, N.H., on February 12 to justify why I should not vote against ratification and/or refute said censure. My nonappearance, the resolution said, would constitute prima facie evidence of my intent to vote for ratification.

Well, I did not go before the caucus, so I have to assume I was tried in absentia and found guilty of a decision I had not yet made at that time.

Now I hope my colleagues are not surprised by the crude message and the abrasive, threatening tone of that resolution of censure. That is the lexicon of the New Right. And it makes a travesty of the movement's efforts to promote itself as respectable and responsible.

Hear, if you will, the revealing words of Howard Phillips on other occasions:

> We organize discontent. We must prove our ability to get revenge on people who go against us. . . . We'll be after them, if they vote the wrong way. We're not going to stop after the vote's past.

And hear the words of another spokesman for the New Right, Paul Weyrich, director of the Committee for the Survival of a Free Congress:

> We are different from previous generations of conservatives. We are no longer working to preserve the status quo. We are radicals, working to overturn the present power structure of this country.

Mr. President, these people are different from traditional conservatives. I know the traditional conservatives of my own state. I have competed with them in the political arena. I have worked with them in behalf of our state. They are people of honor, civility, and decency.

The New Right cannot comprehend how people of opposing viewpoints can find common ground and work together. For them, there is no common ground. And this, in my judgment, is the best indication of what they truly are—radicals whose aim is not to compete with honor and decency, not to compromise when necessary to advance the common good, but to annihilate those they see as enemies.

And if "conservative" in the title "Conservative Caucus" is an ironic misuse of the word, it is doubly ironic that destiny would link the national chairman of the Conservative Caucus—the Governor of New Hampshire—with William Loeb, the publisher of New Hampshire's largest newspaper and the master practitioner of the politics of threat and vengeance.

Within the year, the Governor, the head of the Conservative Caucus, made the following bizarre announcements:

He said the Carter administration was pursuing "a pro-Communist course." He said Martin Luther King "did great harm to the American way of life through his association with Communist-inspired organizations."

In South Africa a few weeks ago, he called our State Department "un-American" but called John Vorster "one of the great world statesmen of today." He said apartheid is a "local South African problem." As for detention without trial in South Africa, he said:

> You know, even Abraham Lincoln suspended habeas corpus during the Civil War.

Fourteen of New Hampshire's top religious leaders issued a joint statement, read from the pulpits of many churches, taking sharp issue with the governor's fawning appraisal of South Africa's leadership and policies. "Our Christian consciences," the clergy said, "will not allow (the governor's) statement to go unanswered."

William Loeb immediately rushed to the governor's defense, declaring in a signed, front page editorial that the fourteen clergymen "have been playing for suckers . . . . Their idealism and their innocence and almost complete ignorance about South Africa has been taken advantage of."

Mr. Loeb went on to give his own appraisal of John Vorster's South African regime. "The South Africans," Loeb said, "are doing the best they can to bring these blacks out of the jungle . . . ."

Mr. President, I cite the above public utterances by the national chairman of the Conservative Caucus and Mr. Loeb only to ask the obvious. If they hold such benighted opinions on those matters, how much credence can we give their views on the Panama Canal treaties?

But credibility may be too much to ask of men whose stock in trade is flag waving, sabre rattling and the politics of threat and vengeance.

In all of this nation, Mr. President, there may not be two more recklessly belligerent public figures than Meldrim Thomson and William Loeb. Though neither has ever worn the uniform of his country into battle, they are the first to demand the kind of precipitous action that could plunge young Americans back into combat.

Only a few weeks after the oil embargo of 1973 got under way, Mr. Loeb charged into this most sensitive situation with an editorial titled: "Let's Go After Our Oil." Calling the Arab leaders "heathen swine," he said that if they did not quickly yield to an embargo and blockade we could ask them, and I quote:

> How would you like to have us bomb your holy cities of Mecca and Medina out of existence?

And not many weeks ago, Governor Thomson went to Taiwan as the guest of that nation and promised that the day would come when the United States would support an invasion of mainland China.

Oddly enough, however, Chairman Thomson's high regard for military power and his willingness to use it is offset by his low esteem of the integrity of military leaders. Listen to his insulting appraisal of why the Joint Chiefs of Staff support the new canal treaties:

"Active commissioned officers," he contends, "will either say what the administration desires or remain silent."

Mr. President, what this notorious armchair warrior—and others like him—is telling us, in effect, is that a man like

Admiral Holloway, a man who fought for his country at Saipan, the Southern Palau Islands, Tinian, Leyte, the Surigao Straits, Korea, and Vietnam, a man who has earned the Bronze Star, the Navy Commendation Medal, the Distinguished Flying Cross and three Air Medals, the US Legion of Merit, and three Distinguished Service Medals, a man who rose to top command of our Navy by the age of fifty-four, cannot be trusted when he tells us, as he did, that "the new treaties are in the best national security interest of the United States."

Mr. President, this is a prime example of what I meant when I said radical extremists believe that we would see every issue as they see it—if there was not something sinister in our motivation. In this instance, the national chairman of the Conservative Caucus—Governor Thomson of New Hampshire—would have us believe that military leaders like Admiral Holloway have compromised their integrity and the nation's security in order to ingratiate themselves with the administration. How insulting. How absurd.

But the beliefs and the tactics of the radical right are nothing new to those of us who call New Hampshire home, Mr. President, so it was no surprise to see Governor Thomson, Mr. Loeb, and the Conservative Caucus team up to threaten vengeance on John Durkin and Tom McIntyre for supporting the canal treaties.

I am certainly not sanguine about such powerful and ruthless opposition, Mr. President, but after sixteen years of weathering the sustained attacks of Mr. Loeb and his ilk neither am I anguishing over the outcome.

My political fate is not my concern here today. My concern is the desperate need for people of conscience and good will to stand up and face down the bully boys of the radical New Right before the politics of intimidation does to America what it has tried to do to New Hampshire.

So I say to my colleagues in closing:

If you want to see the reputations of decent people sullied, stand aside and be silent.

If you want to see people of dignity, integrity, and self-respect refuse to seek public office for fear of what might be conjured or dredged up to attack them or their families, stand aside and be silent.

If you want to see confidential files rifled, informants solicited, universities harassed, "enemy hit lists" drawn up, stand aside and be silent.

If you want to see dissent crushed and expression stifled, stand aside and be silent.

If you want to see the fevered exploitation of a handful of highly emotional issues distract the nation from problems of great consequence, stand aside and be silent.

If you want to see your government deadlocked by rigid intransigence, stand aside and be silent.

If you want this nation held up to worldwide scorn and ridicule because of the outrageous statements and bizarre beliefs of its leaders, stand aside and be silent and let the Howard Phillips, the Meldrim Thomsons and the William Loebs speak for all of us.

Mr. President, I cannot believe that the loutish primitivism of Meldrim Thomson and William Loeb is what the American people want in their leaders, no more than I can believe that the American people want the divisive politics of the radical New Right to determine the course of the nation.

On two occasions in the past several years we witnessed dramatic evidence that the American people desperately want to put acrimony and division aside, to heal the wounds, and to come together again as a people.

The first was that brief and shining moment on Independence Day of our Bicentennial celebration, a moment when all at once we were again united in the pride of our heritage, our esteem and affection for one another, our confidence in the future.

The second occurred but a few short weeks ago when the entire nation paused to pay its final respects to that most beloved of Americans, Hubert Humphrey.

Mr. President, that vast outpouring of admiration and affection for our late colleague was proof enough for me that most Americans want their leaders to be healers—not haters: That most Americans want the politics of mutual respect and good will—not the politics of threat and vengeance; and that most Americans want to be asked for the best that is in them—not the worst.

In the long run, Mr. President, I am confident that the forces of decency and civility will prevail over the politics of intimidation, just as I am confident that reason and commitment rooted in reality will prevail over extremism in the pursuit of illusion.

But if that does not occur in time to save the treaties—or those of us who support them—then I, for one, will go home to Laconia, N.H., sad to leave this office, but content in heart that I voted in what I truly believed were the best interests of my country.

AMERICAN FOREIGN POLICY

OUR COMMON RESPONSIBILITY AND OUR COMMON CHALLENGE[1]

JIMMY CARTER[2]

"Violence, terrorism, assassination, undeclared wars, all threaten to destroy the restraints and moderation that must become the dominant characteristic of our age," said Jimmy Carter to the thirty-second session of the General Assembly of the United Nations, on October 4, 1977. Every seat of the domed Assembly Hall was filled, and many stood along the sides. He was given close attention.

This bleak rhetorical statement represented what responsible leaders from many nations have been saying. In this speech the President set forth his major foreign policy concerns: nuclear proliferation, conventional arms control, peace in Africa, the Arab-Israeli conflict, and the ratification of the treaties with Panama.

The time of the address was significant, for it came the day after the expiration of the five-year nuclear arms accord between the United States and the Soviet Union. The President wished to express the urgency of the situation and at the same time to show optimism about the possibilities of a new agreement on strategic arms limitations (SALT) (Kathleen Teltsch, New York *Times*, October 5, 1977).

During the past year, President Carter and officers in his Administration have devoted much time to foreign affairs. In January, the President made a nine-day, seven-nation, 18,000-mile trip to Poland, Iran, India, Saudi Arabia, Egypt, France, and Belgium. Starting March 28, he made a second trip abroad, covering 14,000 miles in seven days. On this journey he visited Venezuela, Brazil, Nigeria, and Liberia. Although awkward translation detracted from his speeches, particularly in Poland, the President was received warmly and was given considerable television exposure. Secretary of State Cyrus Vance also made important trips abroad to promote peace, and in turn, numerous foreign leaders visited Washington to seek support.

[1] Delivered to the General Assembly of the United Nations, New York City, at 10:30 A.M., October 4, 1977. Title supplied by editor.

[2] For biographical note, see Appendix.

The effectiveness of President Carter in public appearances is debatable. One writer has concluded that "his speeches do not soar, rouse, inspire, enlighten the minds or lift the hearts of his listeners" (Lloyd Shearer, "Intelligence Report," *Parade,* April 16, 1978). James Reston expressed an insightful view of the President:

> He is very persuasive when he is in a small room, expressing his convictions and yearnings to two or three people. Even Chancellor Helmut Schmidt of West Germany testifies to this, but when Mr. Carter talks to a large audience, there is something about his voice and style that loses them, and makes them wonder what he means and where he is going (New York *Times,* April 12, 1978).

Mr. President, Mr. Secretary General, assembled delegates, and distinguished guests:

Mr. President, I wish to offer first my congratulations on your election as President of the 32d General Assembly. It gives my own government particular satisfaction to work under the leadership of a representative from Yugoslavia, a nation with which the United States enjoys close and valued relations.

We pledge our cooperation and will depend heavily on your experience and skill in guiding these discussions which we are beginning.

Mr. President, I would also like to express again the high esteem in which we hold Secretary General Waldheim. We continue to benefit greatly from our close consultations with him, and we place great trust in his leadership of this organization.

Thirty-two years ago, in the cold dawn of the Atomic Age, this organization came into being. Its first and its most urgent purpose has been to secure peace for an exhausted and ravaged world.

Present conditions in some respects appear quite hopeful, yet the assurance of peace continues to elude us. Before the end of this century, a score of nations could possess nuclear weapons. If this should happen, the world that we leave our children will mock our own hopes for peace.

The level of nuclear armaments could grow by tens of thousands, and the same situation could well occur with advanced conventional weapons. The temptation to use these weapons, for fear that someone else might do it first, would be almost irresistible.

The ever-growing trade in conventional arms subverts international commerce from a force for peace to a caterer for war.

Violence, terrorism, assassination, undeclared wars all threaten to destroy the restraint and the moderation that must become the dominant characteristic of our age.

Unless we establish a code of international behavior in which the resort to violence becomes increasingly irrelevant to the pursuit of national interests, we will crush the world's dreams for human development and the full flowering of human freedom.

We have already become a global community, but only in the sense that we face common problems and we share for good or evil a common future. In this community, power to solve the world's problems, particularly economic and political power, no longer lies solely in the hands of a few nations.

Power is now widely shared among many nations with different cultures and different histories and different aspirations. The question is whether we will allow our differences to defeat us or whether we will work together to realize our common hopes for peace.

Today I want to address the major dimensions of peace and the role the United States intends to play in limiting and reducing all armaments, controlling nuclear technology, restricting the arms trade, and settling disputes by peaceful means.

When atomic weapons were used for the first time, Winston Churchill described the power of the atom as a revelation long, mercifully withheld from man. Since then we have learned in Dürrenmatt's chilling words that "what has once been thought can never be un-thought."

If we are to have any assurance that our children are to live out their lives in a world which satisfies our hope—or that they will have a chance to live at all—we must finally come to terms with this enormous nuclear force and turn it exclusively to beneficial ends.

Peace will not be assured until the weapons of war are finally put away. While we work toward that goal, nations will want sufficient arms to preserve their security.

The United States purpose is to insure peace. It is for that reason that our military posture and our alliances will remain as strong as necessary to deter attack. However, the security of the global community cannot forever rest on a balance of terror.

In the past, war has been accepted as the ultimate arbiter of disputes among nations. But in the nuclear era we can no longer think of war as merely a continuation of diplomacy by other means. Nuclear war cannot be measured by the archaic standards of victory or defeat.

This stark reality imposes on the United States and the Soviet Union an awesome and special responsibility. The United States is engaged, along with other nations, in a broad range of negotiations. In strategic arms limitation talks, we and the Soviets are within sight of a significant agreement in limiting the total numbers of weapons and in restricting certain categories of weapons of special concern to each of us. We can also start the crucial process of curbing the relentless march of technological development which makes nuclear weapons ever more difficult to control.

We must look beyond the present and work to prevent the critical threats and instabilities of the future. In the principles of self-restraint, reciprocity, and mutual accommodation of interests, if these are observed, then the United States and the Soviet Union will not only succeed in limiting weapons but will also create a foundation of better relations in other spheres of interest.

The United States is willing to go as far as possible, consistent with our security interest, in limiting and reducing our nuclear weapons. On a reciprocal basis we are willing now to reduce them by ten percent or twenty percent, even fifty percent. Then we will work for further reductions to a world truly free of nuclear weapons.

The United States also recognizes a threat of continued testing of nuclear explosives.

Negotiations for a comprehensive ban on nuclear explosions are now being conducted by the United States, the United Kingdom, and the Soviet Union. As in other areas where vital national security interests are engaged, agreements must be verifiable and fair. They must be seen by all the parties as serving a longer term interest that justifies the restraints of the moment.

The longer term interest in this instance is to close one more avenue of nuclear competition and thereby demonstrate to all the world that the major nuclear powers take seriously our obligations to reduce the threat of nuclear catastrophe.

My country believes that the time has come to end all explosions of nuclear devices, no matter what their claimed justification, peaceful or military, and we appreciate the efforts of other nations to reach this same goal.

During the past nine months, I have expressed the special importance that we attach to controlling nuclear proliferation. But I fear that many do not understand why the United States feels as it does.

Why is it so important to avoid the chance that one or two or ten other nations might acquire one or two or ten nuclear weapons of their own?

Let me try to explain why I deeply believe that this is one of the greatest challenges that we face in the next quarter of a century.

It's a truism that nuclear weapons are a powerful deterrent. They are a deterrent because they threaten. They could be used for terrorism or blackmail as well as for war.

But they threaten not just the intended enemy, they threaten every nation, combatant or noncombatant alike. That is why all of us must be concerned.

Let me be frank. The existence of nuclear weapons in the United States and the Soviet Union, in Great Britain, France, and China, is something that we cannot undo except by the painstaking process of negotiation. But the existence of these weapons does not mean that other nations need to develop their own weapons any more than it provides a reason for those of us who have them to share them with others.

Rather, it imposes two solemn obligations on the nations which have the capacity to export nuclear fuel and nuclear technology—the obligations to meet legitimate energy needs and, in doing so, to insure that nothing that we export contributes directly or indirectly to the production of nuclear explosives. That is why the supplier nations are seeking a common policy, and that is why the United States and the Soviet Union, even as we struggle to find common ground in the SALT talks, have already moved closer toward agreement and cooperation in our efforts to limit nuclear proliferation.

I believe that the London Suppliers Group must conclude its work as it's presently constituted so that the world security will be safeguarded from the pressures of commercial competition. We have learned it is not enough to safeguard just some facilities or some materials. Full-scope, comprehensive safeguards are necessary.

Two weeks from now in our own country, more than thirty supplier and consuming nations will convene for the International Fuel Cycle Evaluation, which we proposed last spring. For the next several years experts will work together on every facet of the nuclear fuel cycle.

The scientists and the policymakers of these nations will face a tremendous challenge. We know that by the year 2000, nuclear power reactors could be producing enough plutonium to make tens of thousands of bombs every year.

I believe from my own personal knowledge of this issue that there are ways to solve the problems that we face. I believe that there are alternative fuel cycles that can be managed safely on a global basis. I hope, therefore, that the International Fuel Cycle Evaluation will have the support and the encouragement of every nation.

I've heard it said that efforts to control nuclear proliferation are futile, that the genie is already out of the bottle. I do not believe this to be true. It should not be forgotten that for twenty-five years the nuclear club did not expand its membership. By genuine cooperation, we can make certain that this terrible club expands no further.

Now, I've talked about the special problems of nuclear arms control and nuclear proliferation at length. Let me turn to the problem of conventional arms control, which affects potentially or directly every nation represented in this great hall. This is not a matter for the future, even the near future, but of the immediate present. Worldwide military expenditures are now in the neighborhood of $300 billion a year.

Last year the nations of the world spent more than 60 times as much—60 times as much—equipping each soldier as we spent educating each child. The industrial nations spent the most money, but the rate of growth in military spending is faster in the developing world.

While only a handful of states produce sophisticated weapons, the number of nations which seek to purchase these weapons is expanding rapidly.

The conventional arms race both causes and feeds on the threat of larger and more deadly wars. It levies an enormous burden on an already troubled world economy.

For our part, the United States has now begun to reduce its arms exports. Our aim is to reduce both the quantity and the deadliness of the weapons that we sell. We have already taken the first few steps, but we cannot go very far alone. Nations whose neighbors are purchasing large quantities of arms feel constrained to do the same. Supplier nations who practice restraint in arms sales sometimes find that they simply lose valuable commercial markets to other suppliers.

We hope to work with other supplier nations to cut back on the flow of arms and to reduce the rate at which the most advanced and sophisticated weapon technologies spread around the world. We do not expect this task to be easy or to produce instant results. But we are committed to stop the spiral of increasing sale of weapons.

Equally important, we hope that purchaser nations, individually and through regional organizations, will limit their arms imports. We are ready to provide to some nations the necessary means for legitimate self-defense, but we are also eager to work with any nation or region in order to decrease the need for more numerous, more deadly, and ever more expensive weapons.

Fourteen years ago one of my predecessors spoke in this very room under circumstances that in certain ways resembled these. It was a time, he said, of comparative calm, and there was an atmosphere of rising hope about the prospect of controlling nuclear energy.

The first specific step had been taken to limit the nuclear arms race—a test ban treaty signed by nearly a hundred nations.

But the succeeding years did not live up to the optimistic prospect John F. Kennedy placed before this assembly, because as a community of nations, we failed to address the deepest sources of potential conflict among us.

As we seek to establish the principles of détente among the major nuclear powers, we believe that these principles must also apply in regional conflicts.

The United States is committed to the peaceful settlement of differences. We are committed to the strengthening of the peacemaking capabilities of the United Nations and regional organizations, such as the Organization of African Unity and the Organization of American States.

The United States supports Great Britain's efforts to

bring about a peaceful, rapid transition to majority rule and independence in Zimbabwe. We have joined other members of the Security Council last week and also the Secretary General in efforts to bring about independence and democratic rule in Namibia. We are pleased with the level of cooperation that we have achieved with the leaders of the nations in the area, as well as those people who are struggling for independence.

We urge South Africa and other nations to support the proposed solution to the problems in Zimbabwe and to cooperate still more closely in providing for a smooth and prompt transition in Namibia. But it is essential that all outside nations exercise restraint in their actions in Zimbabwe and Namibia so that we can bring about this majority rule and avoid a widening war that could engulf the southern half of the African Continent.

Of all the regional conflicts in the world, none holds more menace than the Middle East. War there has already carried the world to the edge of nuclear confrontation. It has already disrupted the world economy and imposed severe hardships on the people in the developed and the developing nations alike.

So, true peace—peace embodied in binding treaties—is essential. It will be in the interest of the Israelis and the Arabs. It is in the interest of the American people. It is in the interest of the entire world.

The United Nations Security Council has provided the basis for peace in Resolutions 242 and 338, but negotiations in good faith by all parties is needed to give substance to peace.

Such good faith negotiations must be inspired by a recognition that all nations in the area—Israel and the Arab countries—have a right to exist in peace, with early establishment of economic and cultural exchange and of normal diplomatic relations. Peace must include a process in which the bitter divisions of generations, even centuries, hatreds and suspicions can be overcome. Negotiations cannot be successful if any of the parties harbor the deceitful view that peace is simply an interlude in which to prepare for war.

Good faith negotiations will also require acceptance by all sides of the fundamental rights and interests of everyone involved.

For Israel this means borders that are recognized and secure. Security arrangements are crucial to a nation that has fought for its survival in each of the last four decades. The commitment of the United States to Israel's security is unquestionable.

For the Arabs, the legitimate rights of the Palestinian people must be recognized. One of the things that binds the American people to Israel is our shared respect for human rights and the courage with which Israel has defended such rights. It is clear that a true and lasting peace in the Middle East must also respect the rights of all peoples of the area. How these rights are to be defined and implemented is, of course, for the interested parties to decide in detailed negotiations and not for us to dictate.

We do not intend to impose, from the outside, a settlement on the nations of the Middle East.

The United States has been meeting with the foreign ministers of Israel and the Arab nations involved in the search for peace. We are staying in close contact with the Soviet Union, with whom we share responsibility for reconvening the Geneva conference.

As a result of these consultations, the Soviet Union and the United States have agreed to call for the resumption of the Geneva conference before the end of this year.

While a number of procedural questions remain, if the parties continue to act in good faith, I believe that these questions can be answered.

The major powers have a special responsibility to act with restraint in areas of the world where they have competing interests, because the association of these interests with local rivalries and conflicts can lead to serious confrontation.

In the Indian Ocean area, neither we nor the Soviet Union has a large military presence, nor is there a rapidly mounting competition between us.

Restraint in the area may well begin with a mutual effort to stabilize our presence and to avoid an escalation in military competition. Then both sides can consider how our military activities in the Indian Ocean, this whole area, might be even further reduced.

The peaceful settlement of differences is, of course, essential. The United States is willing to abide by that principle, as in the case of the recently signed Panama Canal treaties. Once ratified, these treaties can transform the US-Panama relationship into one that permanently protects the interests and respects the sovereignty of both our countries.

We have all survived and surmounted major challenges since the United Nations was founded. But we can accelerate progress even in a world of ever-increasing diversity.

A commitment to strengthen international institutions is vital. But progress lies also in our own national policies. We can work together to form a community of peace if we accept the kind of obligations that I have suggested today.

To summarize: first, an obligation to remove the threat of nuclear weaponry, to reverse the buildup of armaments and their trade, and to conclude bilateral and multilateral arms control agreements that can bring security to all of us. In order to reduce the reliance of nations on nuclear weaponry, I hereby solemnly declare on behalf of the United States that we will not use nuclear weapons except in self-defense; that is, in circumstances of an actual nuclear or conventional attack on the United States, our territories, or armed forces, or such an attack on our allies.

In addition, we hope that initiatives by the Western nations to secure mutual and balanced force reductions in Europe will be met by equal response from the Warsaw Pact countries.

Second, an obligation to show restraint in areas of tension, to negotiate disputes and settle them peacefully, and to strengthen peacemaking capabilities of the United Nations and regional organizations.

And finally, an effort by all nations, east as well as west, north as well as south, to fulfill mankind's aspirations for human development and human freedom. It is to meet these basic demands that we build governments and seek peace.

We must share these obligations for our own mutual survival and our own mutual prosperity.

We can see a world at peace. We can work for a world without want. We can build a global community dedicated to these purposes and to human dignity.

The view that I have sketched for you today is that of only one leader in only one nation. However wealthy and powerful the United States may be, however capable of leadership, this power is increasingly only relative. The leadership increasingly is in need of being shared.

No nation has a monopoly of vision, of creativity, or of ideas. Bringing these together from many nations is our common responsibility and our common challenge. For only in these ways can the idea of a peaceful global community grow and prosper.

HUMAN RIGHTS AND DÉTENTE[3]

ARTHUR J. GOLDBERG[4]

On October 6, 1977, Arthur J. Goldberg, US Ambassador-at-Large and chairman of the US Delegation to the Conference on Security and Cooperation in Europe (CSCE), spoke to the delegates of the thirty-five signatories of the 1975 Helsinki Accord, meeting in Belgrade, Yugoslavia. The main business before the conference was to review compliance of the members with the accord signed two years before at the end of the Conference on European Security and Cooperation in Helsinki, Finland.

The Helsinki Accord, as the 1975 Final Act is known, was not a treaty and had "no binding force on the United States, the Soviet Union or the other nations," but "it has become a yardstick against which to measure progress in improving east-west relations." It provided "a framework for adjusting east-west differences in trade and commercial matters and in humanitarian and information-flow practices." Further, it made possible and appropriate for one sovereign state to question another on human rights and on "compliance with international standards of conduct toward political and religious expression" (Representative Dante B. Fascell, Democrat from Florida, *Congressional Record,* October 20, 1977, p H11373).

Ambassador Goldberg presented the formal position of the United States on matters to come before the conference. What he said did not constitute a great speech, but it was an important one because the Administration had made human rights an important plank in American foreign policy (see Cyrus R. Vance's "Human Rights and the Foreign Policy," REPRESENTATIVE AMERICAN SPEECHES: 1976-1977, p 127-37). Probably the most knowledgeable State Department officials and presidential assistants advised Goldberg on what to include in his text. They attempted to balance American objectives against Soviet interests and the visionary against the attainable. They knew that the stakes could be high and the outcome might well depend upon the Goldberg spoken rhetoric and delivery. This speech was more than a reflection of its

[3] Delivered to the Conference on Security and Cooperation in Europe, Belgrade, Yugoslavia, October 6, 1977. Quoted by permission.

[4] For biographical note, see Appendix.

speaker; it was a declaration of US foreign policy by well-informed advisers on American foreign affairs.

Unfortunately, speeches of this type often have an anemic quality and are seldom noteworthy for eloquence or magnificent delivery. They are usually filled with generalizations and imperatives; they are expressed in carefully selected words that are precise and not equivocal. They omit specific examples, evidence, and amplificatory passages. As one writer said, Goldberg is "determined not to mute the human rights cause to the point of inaudibility, even if he does sound off with aggressive trumpeting" (Flora Lewis, New York *Times,* October 16, 1977).

Mr. Chairman, fellow delegates, on behalf of the American delegation, permit me to express our sincere thanks to our hosts, the government of Yugoslavia. We are more than grateful for the facilities and support they have so generously provided for the conduct of our work. It is particularly symbolic that this conference is held in a nation which has done so much for so long to promote security and cooperation in Europe.

Two years and two months ago the leaders of our thirty-five nations assembled in Helsinki to conclude—with their solemn approval—the Final Act of the Conference on Security and Cooperation in Europe.

This week we are beginning in Belgrade a new phase of the process they initiated. We are embarking on a mutual examination of our experiences in implementing the Final Act. We are also seeking together new means of solidifying and building from the foundations laid in Helsinki.

Our task is part of a great and ancient enterprise: the search for security, the advancement of cooperation in Europe. This conference is one more step toward that high goal, one part of the broader process of reducing risks of confrontation in Europe and of replacing them with opportunities for cooperation.

This meeting is both an expression and a result of considerable improvements in east-west relations. In turn, what we accomplish here in the coming months can have a direct impact on the further development of détente.

I have been designated by President Carter to speak here as the representative of the United States Secretary of State. I carry with me the President's deep, personal commitment to advance the goals of the Final Act and the work of which it is such an important element. He is dedicated to working constructively with all nations represented here, to help fulfill the Final Act's commitment to improved European security and cooperation.

Two corollary principles make the Helsinki approach unique. One is our rule of consensus, the recognition that every nation should take part on an equal footing in decisions which affect the future of Europe. The second is also crucial: the tie, formalized by the Final Act, between the freedom and welfare of each of our nations, and the freedom and welfare of each of our individual citizens. Let me reaffirm in the most positive terms the wholehearted commitment of the United States government to the pursuit of détente. Let me also restate our view that a deepening of détente, a healing of the divisions in Europe, cannot be divorced from progress in humanitarian matters and human rights. The pursuit of human rights does not put détente in jeopardy. Rather, it can strengthen détente and provide a firmer basis for both security and cooperation.

The United States wants to build upon and enlarge the scope of east-west understanding. For my government is convinced that this conference in Belgrade must not be the end of the CSCE process. Rather, it must be an occasion to inject fresh momentum into that process. The true test of the work we do together lies not only in the conclusions we reach. It lies also in the higher goals we set and in the energy with which we set about meeting them.

My government will do its best to provide new impetus to the CSCE process, both here in Belgrade and in our overall policies towards Europe and the world.

We will conduct the review of implementation on the basis of the unity of all sections of the Final Act and the equal value of all the principles.

We will make clear our intention to honor the political commitments in this document and to utilize fully the practical opportunities it opens.

We will discuss concrete problems, of both past and future implementation.

And we will conduct our policies in Europe fully aware of the fact that CSCE can only bear part of the burden for guarding the peace. There must also be progress in other efforts at détente; and the benefits of our efforts must be applied throughout Europe. Berlin, for example, remains a basic testing place of détente. This divided city must continue to receive the benefits of the Final Act. Berlin must prosper under the Quadripartite Agreement, free from crisis, if détente and CSCE are to succeed.

Just as the United States goal for Europe is one of peace, so at this conference we seek no confrontation. We have no desire to trade debating points. Instead, we want to exchange ideas on how better to implement the Final Act. We seek a thorough, non-polemical, straightforward, and detailed review of implementation. And through that review, we seek to help formulate new measures which can give added concrete expression and momentum to the basic commitments of the Final Act.

General Assessment

The first obligation we all share is to conduct a candid review of the promises each of us has made, the promises we have kept, and the promises we have yet to fulfill.

The assessment my country has made of the overall record of participating states over the last twenty-six months shows encouraging evidence of progress. But the progress displayed is not progress enough. It still falls short of the goals of the Final Act and, just as important, of the high expectations the Final Act aroused. Those expectations remain valid, and we must all be frank in judging that many of them remain unmet.

Let me comment first on what my own country has done

to implement the Final Act. In general, the Act codified standards which reflect American policy in dealing with other nations and with our own citizens. Nevertheless, in response to the Final Act we have looked closely at our own behavior and—where we have found the need and the means—have acted to improve our conduct. In particular, we took two steps regarding the Final Act pledge to "facilitate freer movement and contacts." First, President Carter this year removed all restrictions on travel abroad by American citizens. Second, with President Carter's support, Congress recently relaxed our visa requirements, so that people wishing to visit the United States will not be excluded because of political affiliation or belief, except in the rarest instances.

Moreover, in the field of human rights, President Carter yesterday redeemed a pledge he gave last spring by signing the International Covenants on Human Rights at the United Nations. American adherence to those pacts has been a matter of personal concern to me and to many others for a decade.

The President is pledged to pursue ratification of the Covenants. Meanwhile, his action yesterday is in earnest of our good faith and a proof of the positive impact the Final Act is having in the United States.

In the spheres of commercial, cultural, educational and scientific exchanges, we have done much and have much yet to do. For example, the United States government has made a special effort to inform our businessmen about provisions of the Final Act affecting their opportunities to enter and work in markets with which they have not always been sufficiently familiar. This year, we signed our first cultural, educational, and scientific cooperation agreements with Hungary and Bulgaria; and we concluded negotiations on a similar agreement with Czechoslovakia. With the Soviet Union, we renewed several scientific cooperation arrangements.

Meanwhile, in some other signatory nations, we have seen a well-intentioned and productive effort to implement the principles and provisions of the Final Act. In some nations in the east, advances have been only modest, and are still far below the Final Act's standards. And there are individual cases under the Final Act where forward motion has been stalled or even reversed.

Under the stimulus of the Final Act, some progress has been made in bettering relations among the participating states. The exchange of goods, knowledge, people, and ideas has expanded in some measure. Substantial obstacles do remain to travel and the flow of information between one part of Europe and another, but these have already diminished somewhat. This improvement can be seen simply in the numbers of people who have been able to leave old homes for new ones in Europe, America, and Israel. These results mean real individual happiness, and we here must reaffirm our resolve to speed that development.

Likewise, in translating our shared political undertakings to the area of military security, the Final Act has brought another kind of exchange, promising but incomplete. Confidence-building measures, involving advance notification of maneuvers and exchange of observers, have made openness a virtue in a field where secrecy was once instinctive. We have laid a foundation on which this meeting can productively build.

Thus we can see some progress.

We can see it in terms of individuals and families reunited after being separated by war, accident, and history. But we must recall the many who remain apart.

We can see progress in business contacts that become business contracts. But we cannot overlook the still inadequate supply of relevant economic data on which the growth of business confidence depends.

We can see progress in books translated, performers applauded, students instructed, and scientific theories tested. But here, too, the openness and ease of contact promised at Helsinki has been only partly realized.

Thus, we cannot be satisfied with the record of implementation. The standard we have set together should be even higher, if the goals of the Final Act are to be realized.

Let me illustrate some areas in which we in the United States feel old practices have not been changed sufficiently to meet the new imperatives of the Helsinki spirit.

In educational exchange programs, it is not enough to increase the number of scholars involved; rather, a prerequisite for such an increase is improved freedom for scholars and their research. What value is there, for example, in financing a student's work abroad, when for months he is denied admission to an essential archive, and when, having finally been admitted one day, he is not permitted back the next—even to collect his notes?

Also, in seeking "to facilitate the freer and wider dissemination of information of all kinds," we cannot point convincingly to progress while international broadcasts are subjected to continuing interference.

Similarly, while steps have been taken to ease travel and working conditions for journalists, these advances are jeopardized when visas are made conditional on a correspondent's agreeing to contact certain sources of information and opinion.

Finally, while real progress has been made in reuniting divided families and concluding binational marriages, satisfaction with those developments must be balanced by regret that many long-standing cases remain unresolved, that the resolution of routine cases is too often arbitrary and capricious, and that new bureaucratic obstacles are imposed on people seeking to join relatives abroad. This runs counter to the Helsinki promise "gradually to simplify" exit procedures. It is also hard to see the workings of the "positive and humanitarian spirit" when an ill and aged husband is denied, after long years of separation, the company of his nearly blind wife and their daughter.

Equally difficult to understand are broader restrictions on the right of individuals to travel or emigrate. That right is established in Article 13 of the Universal Declaration of

Human Rights: "Everyone has the right to leave any country, including his own, and to return to his country." All of us have pledged in the Final Act to "act in conformity" with that Universal Declaration, and we have given specific emphasis to that promise in the Final Act's provisions on family reunification.

Human Rights and Détente

The two years since the Helsinki summit are particularly short when we set them against the historic divisions we are trying, through the Final Act, to bridge. Some of the deepest differences among the participating states lie in views on the status of the individual in relation to the state. The issue of human rights represents the widest gap between the ideals and practices of east and west. It is a sensitive subject on the international agenda, but one which can be dealt with in an understanding manner, and which must be discussed in order to facilitate further progress under the Final Act.

Precisely because the distance between our views on human rights is so great, we must all work to narrow the divide. This is not a simple process. In my own country, a mere fifteen years ago many Americans were denied the right to vote. But through commitment to an ideal, and constant efforts to reach that ideal, this blemish on the American record was removed. Other serious blemishes remain, and our efforts to remove them also remain constant. The process is inevitably a gradual one, but efforts like ours are what make progress in human rights possible under the Final Act.

In the United States, we also realize that human rights encompass economic and social rights as well as political and civil liberties. It is our view that one set of values cannot be stressed at the expense of the other. Rather, it is the combination of these rights and the respect in which governments hold them all which offer the best promise that all can be attained.

Concern for these rights is not new either to Americans or to the other states taking part in this Conference. It is enshrined in Article 1 of the Charter of the United Nations. It is enshrined in the Universal Declaration of Human Rights. And the Final Act, in Principle VII, binds all the participating states to "recognize the universal significance of human rights and fundamental freedoms, respect for which is an essential factor for the peace, justice and well-being necessary to ensure the development of friendly relations and cooperation among themselves as among all states."

American policy—evolving from a history of political development with deep roots here in Europe, and nurtured by the efforts of other nations—has long pursued that vision. It is explicit in our Bill of Rights. It animated the Four Freedoms proclaimed by President Franklin Roosevelt—freedom from want and fear, freedom of speech and religion—for which Americans last fought on this continent in the war against fascism. It was also part of the heritage of President Kennedy when, fourteen years ago, he launched a fresh initiative for world peace. He asked: "Is not peace in the last analysis a matter of human rights?" And he proposed an "agreement on a freer flow of information and people from East to West and West to East."

When such an agreement was concluded in Helsinki as part of the Final Act, President Ford echoed his predecessors' words. He said: "The founders of my country did not merely say that all Americans should have these rights, but all men everywhere should have these rights."

On many occasions this year, President Carter has set forth his own commitment to the continuity of American policy in the area of human rights—whether political, economic, social, or cultural. At the United Nations last March, he stressed that the "search for peace also means the justice . . . (and) the search for peace and justice means also respect for human dignity . . . I know perhaps as well as anyone that our ideals in the area of human rights have not always been attained in the United States, but the American people have an abiding commitment to the full realization of these ideals. We are determined therefore to deal with our deficiencies quickly and openly."

It is in that same spirit that the United States delegation will speak about human rights and basic freedoms here in Belgrade. We have much to learn from that exchange of views.

Let me illustrate some of our concerns. The Principle VII guarantee of religion and belief means to us that expression of faith must not be penalized by loss or reduction of educational or career opportunities. People should be free to worship without fear or state interference in their choice of ministers, literature, and houses of prayer.

Similarly, the "freedom of thought and conscience" we have all pledged to respect must have breathing space in which to flourish. Its expression should not be censored. Its exponents should not be imprisoned or exiled for making their thoughts known.

Moreover, the "legitimate interests" of "national minorities in our thirty-five states require respect for unique cultural and linguistic heritages, and active policies to preserve these traditions and achievements for future generations.

Our governments have assumed the responsibility to "promote and encourage the effective exercise" of these rights. And in Principle VII we subscribed to "the right of the individual to know and act upon his rights and duties" in the field of human rights. The response of citizens to that challenge, alone and in either private or public groupings in many signatory states, has been heartening evidence of the Final Act's healthy impact on all of us. In my own country, we have benefited by the dedication, candor, and commitment of our Commission on Security and Cooperation in Europe. Its valuable work will be reflected in what we do here in Belgrade; and we are honored by having its members as part of our delegation.

All the more, then, we are also obliged to register vigorous disapproval of repressive measures taken in any country against individuals and private groups whose activities relate solely to promoting the Final Act's goals and promises.

And such repression is contrary to the spirit and the letter of our common pledge. Rather, at this meeting, we should all reaffirm the valuable role to be played by individuals and organizations, in their own countries and in international associations, to help make that pledge a reality.

Conclusion

In the coming weeks, the United States delegation will focus its efforts in a constructive manner on improving relations among the participating states. We are here to help strengthen prospects for cooperation, and to help move closer towards what should be the noblest common goal of this Conference: to give the process of détente a human measure and a humanitarian face.

In that spirit, the United States delegation will consider and, as appropriate, support new measures to improve implementation of the Final Act. We see opportunities for improvement in the following areas:

Promotion of human rights;

Execution of confidence-building measures;

Qualitative expansion of scientific, economic and commercial data exchanges;

Easing of travel for journalists and businessmen;

Freer access to printed and broadcast information from other countries; and

Fuller opportunities for scholars and scholarship.

This list by no means exhausts our agenda or the specific ideas the United States, with other interested states, will pursue in the coming months. There are also opportunities to promote the exchange of literature, television programs, and culture of all kinds. There are possibilities for exploring, in such appropriate agencies as the UN Economic Commission for Europe, the coordination of approaches to such pervasive problems as environmental pollution. And, there is great potential for expanding trade and for sharing the benefits of technology.

However, our success will be measured not solely by words on paper, but rather by what we all do both here and at home after this meeting ends. Together we must give the process of implementation direction, higher goals, and fresh momentum, to ensure that—when we next meet in a similar assembly—we can record even greater progress.

In our work we will need patience, perseverance and perspective. This Conference in Belgrade is one stage of a dynamic process and a continuing dialogue. And that Helsinki process is part of an even larger effort to build more secure and more humane relations among our nations and peoples.

We are nearer the beginning than the end. The Conference must give the people of the signatory countries and people throughout the world a first report of first progress. It must demonstrate to them our shared commitment to go further. We owe them our best efforts and results better than those so far achieved.

SCIENCE AND MAN'S FUTURE

SCIENCE AND THE LAW[1]

WILLIAM J. MCGILL[2]

Recently, Americans, longing for a return to the simple life, have been near hysteria over problems that seem to originate from scientific and technological development. Consumers have been aroused by what William J. McGill, president of Columbia University, has referred to as "the conflict-oriented style of mass media" and what overzealous investigative reporters tend to emphasize. The newspapers and airways have been filled with reports of oil spills, cancer-producing substances, air and water pollution, nuclear proliferation, poisoning of chemical workers, ozone-depleting aerosol cans, fish kills, overuse of chemical fertilizers, unwise disposal of waste materials, and possibly hazardous research on recombinant DNA. Each new problem has won the support of a well-financed pressure group eager to secure injunctions from the courts.

William J. McGill summarized this near-hysteria, saying:

> A deepening cynicism and almost paranoid mistrust of established institutions appear to have gripped the American people in the aftermath of the Vietnam war and the Watergate scandals. Fortunately the courts have emerged from this troubled period with enhanced respect. But the burden of conflict resolution which the legal profession and our courts are now expected to bear has also increased geometrically. It raises serious doubts about the capacity of our legal system to deal effectively with public discord on the scale projected by the recent growth of adversary conflict in the United States.

McGill delivered his speech September 20, 1977, at a dinner held at the Waldorf Astoria Hotel in New York City by the Guild of Catholic Lawyers of the Archdiocese of New York. As he indicated in his introduction and conclusion, the occasion marked

[1] Delivered to the Guild of Catholic Lawyers of the Archdiocese of New York, meeting at the Waldorf Astoria Hotel, New York City, September 20, 1977. Quoted by permission of William J. McGill and *Change Magazine*.

[2] For biographical note, see Appendix.

the five-hundreth anniversary of the birth of St. Thomas More (1478-1535), English statesman, author, and churchman, as well as the golden anniversary of the foundation of the guild. Prior to the dinner the guild had sponsored its annual Red Mass at St. Patrick's Cathedral with Terence Cardinal Cooke as the principal concelebrant.

The president of a great university, McGill told his audience of lawyers how the problem of public intervention touches his institution: "The use of the adversary legal process to control scientific research is likely to lead to serious scientific error and to badly thought-out policy." In a solution that deserves thoughtful consideration, McGill suggested that ways must be found to monitor science in areas that threaten life, but that the uninformed and hysterical must not be permitted to block progress needed to keep pace with a more complex world and an ever-increasing demand.

The speech received wide attention. An article based upon it appeared in *Change Magazine* (December 1977), an excerpt was printed in *Science,* published by the American Association for the Advancement of Science (October 21, 1977), and the full speech was included in *Vital Speeches of the Day* (October 15, 1977).

It is a great honor for me to have been invited here this evening at the outset of the fiftieth anniversary of the founding of the Guild of Catholic Lawyers of the Archdiocese of New York. The time appears also to coincide with the five hundredth anniversary of the birth of Saint Thomas More, the remarkably courageous Lord Chancellor of England whose resistance to the Act of Supremacy separating the English Church from Rome, and whose ultimate martyrdom at the hand of Henry VIII, have made him the patron saint of lawyers. It is easy to feel intimidated by both the historical setting and the professional competence of this distinguished audience.

My only serious legal qualification to address you is the fact that during the nearly eight years in which I have served as president of Columbia University, I have been sued and investigated repeatedly for attempting to carry out the duties which the trustees assigned to me. I cannot claim to be overscrupulous, but I would also never consider crossing the street against a red light. I do not smoke, although my wife does. And when she opens a pack of cigarettes, I see to it always that she tears the tax stamp. I drive our automobile very carefully never exceeding the speed limit and would certainly consider it unthinkable to violate the eight-foot law. Yet the events of the last ten years in California and in New York have managed to lose for me the status I once enjoyed as an untarnished legal virgin. I have found myself on the receiving end of more than a hundred lawsuits and at least one state legislative investigation.

It is perhaps indicative of the current conditions of life for university presidents that I find myself casting my eye warily around the room searching for problems beyond those of which I am already aware. I see at least a dozen familiar faces, distinguished attorneys with whom I have been recently involved, or perhaps the correct word is embroiled. Out of respect for the rules of Marquess of Queensberry no one has served a legal paper on me this evening—at least not yet!

Seriously, I want to speak to you this evening about the increasingly adversary character of American public life as it affects the administration of science. It is not quite true that all of us are threatening to sue the pants off each other or to investigate the daylights out of one another, but it is also not ludicrously false either. In the years since World War II the mass media of communication in the United States have greatly enhanced our nation's almost unlimited capacity for disputatiousness. Of course it is not a new problem. Conflict is what sells newspapers, and more than seventy years ago Roscoe Pound called attention to America's unusual legal contentiousness in a remarkable paper on the causes of popular dissatisfaction with the administration of justice. Nevertheless, with the conflict-oriented style of our mass media, and present day judicial standards for redressing grievances, we seem to be moving to a more distilled form of purely adversary society than even Dean Pound foresaw.

The emerging social order in America may well be one

in which policy at all levels is forged from the clash of narrowly based constituency interests, each one at war for its own special advantage without regard for the others or for the larger public interest. US visitors to the People's Republic of China have commented on the striking differences between modern China and modern America in this respect. China is well-organized and harmonious, displaying a universal popular dedication to the growth of its brand of rigorous Marxism, whereas the United States carries on its business in a continuing swirl of investigations, legal actions, inflated rhetoric, criticism in the newspapers, and other pressures.

I certainly do not want to be naive about this problem. The subtleties of another culture are easily misunderstood nor is it immediately evident that harmony achieved by suppression of dissent is preferable to the hurly-burly of American public life. Dispute is a trivial price to pay for the benefits of a free society, but frankly I am worried about the effects of these psychological stresses on our people. A deepening cynicism and almost paranoid mistrust of established institutions appear to have gripped the American people in the aftermath of the Vietnam war and the Watergate scandals. Fortunately the courts have emerged from this troubled period with enhanced respect. But the burden of conflict resolution which the legal profession and our courts are now expected to bear has also increased geometrically. It raises serious doubts about the capacity of our legal system to deal effectively with public discord on the scale projected by the recent growth of adversary conflict in the United States.

I hope I will not be misunderstood if I say that these developments seem to me to have occurred in direct proportion to the willingness of the courts to intervene in the operation of our society's institutions. We live in an era of extraordinary judicial activism in which the courts have shown themselves quite prepared to administer schools, prison systems, state police organizations, municipal services, and many other institutional activities, if deemed necessary to achieve compliance with their orders.

It may indeed be necessary. And legislatures have shown no alarm about this remarkable expansion of judicial power. Indeed they have encouraged it, and have themselves produced a burgeoning regulatory apparatus performing quasi-judicial functions even more interventionist than our courts in its approach to society's other institutions. Americans are above all impatient. Our legal system seems to prefer social change by direct intervention into the functioning of businesses, schools, local government, and other institutions rather than through the patient application of correctives or incentives.

We ought to think more seriously about such developments. Although legal contentiousness is an old problem in the United States, large-scale judicial intervention is of fairly recent origin. There is now a substantive basis for complaint by the business sector that the interventionist bent of the courts and the government is making it increasingly difficult to form capital, thus unwittingly but effectively altering the nature of our economic system. Similarly there is a growing basis for complaint by the institutional nonprofit sector of society: schools, colleges, hospitals, churches, and social agencies to the effect that the interventionist bent of the courts and the regulatory agencies has so embroiled these institutions in community struggle that our traditional commitments to intellectual and moral excellence have had to be suppressed in order to meet the priorities of peacemaking.

I do not rise before you this evening merely to offer expression to the frustrations that every chief administrator of a major American university feels in attempting to guide his own institution safely through this Darwinian imbroglio. When we alter the power relations in society, frustrations must be expected. Institutions cannot continue to operate in their traditional easy ways because profound changes are occurring in American life. They have altered the power relations among the components of society to an astonishing extent and there will be no ease for those who carry administrative responsibility. The point of my initial argument is that I do not accept the view of many lawyers and judges with whom I have discussed this problem, that they are more or less passive observers of society's disputes; that all this is part of the history and sociology of our time.

There is no doubt in my mind that a causal sequence exists linking the willingness of the courts to review the decisions of university administrators with the development of new legislation attempting to influence the outcome of such reviews, and that both these factors tend to increase the number of disputes at universities that eventually find their way into court. It appears to me that the social process by which this causal sequence occurs is obvious and that courts and legislatures should not deceive themselves about the consequences of their activism. They are shapers of society, not passive arbiters.

In part the difficulties I am describing are the growing pains of a vigorous and creative free people. Repression of dissent and rigorous planning are as foreign to the dramatics of current American life as they seem to be natural in the Marxist states. It is plausible to argue that legislative and judicial interventionism in the US has prevented the growth of revolutionary forces by giving voice to segments of our society previously excluded from decision-making. I happen to believe that, but I am also charged with the guidance of one of the great educational institutions of the world, and I have to tell you that the character of the community struggles in which I find myself continuously enmeshed, makes me wonder how in the world we ever make sensible educational decisions. It is a question of balance and proportion. In recent years the balance has been struck in such a way as to involve us regularly with militant advocacy groups which object to our educational activities and move quite effectively to influence them.

It is plain that this adversary pushing and shoving may be either good or bad depending on the nature of the dangers which our centers of thought and research pose to society, as well as on the extremely subtle question of what the first concerns of a university ought to be. If in the long run this turbulent era is seen as strengthening America by broadening the base of our democracy, increasing our respect for law, and preventing social harm, then the frustrations which we university administrators now endure will have been well worth it. On the other hand, it is not difficult to argue that we are weakening America's scientific leadership by unwittingly establishing the principle that the conflicting advocacy of the legislature or the courtroom is the best way to develop sound public policy in science and technology. I want to develop this point with you briefly this evening and I want to counsel forbearance.

In many parts of the country a serious town-gown struggle is developing between universities and their surrounding communities over research on recombinant DNA. The basic knowledge and biochemical technology have been developed by which scientists can combine segments of genetic material from different molecules. Thus DNA molecules can be generated in the laboratory that are not known to exist in nature. These new research techniques also make it possible to transfer laboratory-generated genetic material to host cells where it seems to be able to replicate itself and actually to function. An immensely powerful research tool has thus been created offering untold possibilities for understanding the nature of life processes and for the production of desirable biological substances, scarce hormones for example. It also offers the possibility of inadvertently creating biological hazards. One of the methods involves the introduction of foreign genes into known viruses. A potentially lethal virus might be created. The spectre is raised of the escape of an artificially generated uncontrollable disease. Biologists acknowledge that it is not possible to give absolute assurances on this dangerous outcome, but they rate the probability as vanishingly small if the research is properly administered and carried out by people who know what they are doing. The overwhelming majority of biologists believe that the research must be undertaken because it is the avenue to new basic knowledge. The human race cannot protect itself by hiding from discovery. Most biologists are certain that the risks are controllable. They themselves proposed the safety standards now enforced by the National Institutes of Health to deal with biohazards.

All this was done before the general public had become aware of the nature of the problem. The biological research community performed a notable public service in seeking to develop public awareness and understanding of the biohazards associated with research on DNA. But the discussion has begun to cause deep apprehensions among well-educated and intelligent representatives of the general public. Serious efforts to suppress the research are now being undertaken by opponents who fear some form of permanent damage to the human race.

One of the most attractive aspects of the era in which we live is the great public concern for the preservation of our natural environment. This concern has manifested itself in a veritable maze of statutory and regulatory constraints on industrial technology. No industrial process in the United States can dump its waste products into the air or into a body of water without reprocessing the waste to eliminate pollution. Dumping practices which were quite widespread only two decades ago are rapidly disappearing under rigorous public control and tough legislation. No one yet knows how much of such regulation might be reasonably described as excessive. Pollution control typically adds to the costs of industrial processes and such costs are invariably passed along to consumers. The adversary process of the courtroom is being employed to develop the essential truths about the relation between a clean environment as defined by statute and the cost of achieving it.

The struggle has spawned large numbers of public interest groups which seek out and identify the major offenders, develop the evidence against industrial polluters, and eventually bring the cases into court. The courts have responded by attempting to set well-defined guidelines and timetables in areas of environmental protection in which the technical data are not yet fully understood. The law here is quite undeveloped. Anti-pollution advocates are constantly searching for new problems so that they might alert the public to the dangers and move in court to protect the public safety.

The methods used were perfected during the civil rights movement. They involve a unique combination of legal attack and clever public relations. The mass media are used extensively in order to achieve a favorable impact on public opinion. The publicity puts great pressure on the businesses charged with environmental carelessness. Hence many of the actions move quickly to a negotiated settlement in order to prevent legislation that might be even more damaging than the negotiated outcome. The methods are uniquely matched to the achievement of desirable objectives in a democratic society and I have nothing but admiration for them. Moreover, they are very potent. The combination of threatened lawsuits, and reams of publicity hinting that a firm is responsible for injuries or deaths because of an unreasonable concern for profit has done wonders in bringing industrial polluters to heel.

Much of this legal and publicity apparatus has now been turned upon the scientific community and upon research on recombinant DNA. We are seeing the familiar combination of legal pressures and fear-arousal through hysterical newspaper coverage.

There is no rule of advocacy restricting claims about the potential dangers of DNA to those which have some basis in scientific reasoning. As a consequence, dramatic overstatement, innuendo, and purple rhetoric, the familiar tools of the adversary process of the courtroom, have combined virtually to bury the facts on DNA in a mass of fear and confusion. There is a real danger that fearful communities will seek to regulate scientific research at the lowest level of our political governance where serious thought and careful analysis are often lacking. The City Council of Cambridge, Massachusetts, has already interposed itself as the regulator of potentially hazardous biological research at Harvard and MIT. The Attorney General of the state of New York and the City Council are considering the same kind of control here. Plainly these bodies know next to nothing about either the dangers or the subtleties of biological research. Their approach is a purely political one, responding to the fears of the voters. To those of us raised in the traditions of academic freedom the atmosphere is reminiscent of the days of Galileo and the Inquisition.

If any one in this audience believes that I am myself falling victim to overstatement and purple rhetoric in hinting of a possible revival of the Inquisition, let me note that in 1963 Columbia University applied for a permit to operate a 250-kilowatt Triga nuclear reactor as a training device for its engineering students. The permit was opposed by community groups on the ground that the proposed installation constituted a radiation hazard to the densely populated surrounding area on Morningside Heights. I should note that 250 kilowatts is much less power than it takes to light the campus at night. The Triga reactor is a rather simple training device which has been judged to be completely safe by committees of competent scientists at Columbia and elsewhere, but these considerations do not diminish public apprehensions that we are somehow dumping lethal radiation on our innocent neighbors.

Community opposition initially took the form of intervention in the university's application for a license to operate the research reactor. During nearly a decade of struggle before hearing and review boards of the Atomic Energy Commission, the safety issue was studied in a legal record that eventually accumulated many thousands of pages. Finally in 1972 the AEC concluded its hearing procedures and announced its intention to issue a license. The intervenors promptly took the federal government to court with Columbia as an interested bystander. During all this time the device remained inoperative. In 1973 the Federal Appeals Court of the Second District of New York ruled the Columbia reactor safe and authorized the issuance of a federal license to operate it. The intervenors then brought the matter to the US Supreme Court. In 1974 the court refused to review the decision of the Second District and the matter was finally settled. Columbia was then free at last to obtain a license to operate its training reactor. The license was issued in 1977.

Now that should end the story—right? Wrong! Following the Supreme Court's action on licensing, opponents of the Columbia reactor introduced prohibition bills in the state legislature and the New York City Council. The City Council ruled that a permit from the Health Department would be required. We applied. The permit was denied citing the same environmental safety arguments rejected by the Federal Court of Appeals. We are now once more back in court, this time side by side with the federal government arguing that the city's health permit improperly contravenes the federal licensing authority. No doubt this case too will be appealed up the line to the highest courts, and perhaps some day a future generation of Columbia students may be able to benefit from the training available at forty-four such installations in this country and abroad.

The essential point is that we are now in the fifteenth year of our effort to carry on research and training in nuclear engineering at Columbia, and thus far, although we have won every legal argument, the reactor continues inoperative. I ask you whether or not this activity has been effectively suppressed at Columbia?

The intervenors put forth a list of quasi-scientific arguments calculated to impress lawyers and judges but which leave our scientists baffled. So-called "expert" academic witnesses were brought into court claiming that similar nuclear research devices have altered the frequency of birth defects in surrounding communities elsewhere in the country. Our scientists have studied the data and pronounced them phoney—cooked up for legal argument and without scientific merit. How is one to judge who is right? Isn't it safer to suppress the research in view of all the opposition, and in virtue of the admittedly slim but conceivable possibility that there may be some real danger? This is what my legislative friends tell me, but unfortunately our engineers and physicists have just as strong a claim to the protections of academic freedom as philosophers have. Hence we cannot accept an outcome that is scientifically wrong even though it may be politically expedient.

I have gone through the development of this case history in some detail so as to argue that the most probable outcome of the adversary process in issue involving the safety of scientific research is prolonged suppression of the research.

The conflicting advocacy of the courtroom unfortunately does not contribute effectively to the understanding of these extremely subtle scientific questions. The issues are always highly technical, turning on a level of knowledge and scientific judgment not easily transplanted from the laboratory. The adversary method for arriving at truth on which our legal procedures are based is, in simple language, not appropriate for arriving at sound policy on scientific matters. Scientific questions simply cannot be settled by persuasive argument.

The only effective method for resolving safety questions in nuclear or biological research is the objective analysis of experimental results by our best scientific minds. It is not a harmonious process by any means, but it is the only way to arrive at sensible judgments about the meaning of research findings.

What I am saying, in unvarnished simplicity, is that the use of the adversary legal process to control scientific research is likely to lead to serious scientific errors and to badly thought-out policy. The protracted denial of an important research tool in nuclear engineering to Columbia's students will not damage the university fatally. We shall manage, but an extension of the same principle to attempted public control of research in biology, physics, and chemistry, would be a destructive policy. This kind of control should be exercised only in the most extreme circumstances when universities show themselves to be unable to take reasonable steps on behalf of public safety. Public control is especially worrisome when it is exercised by district courts or local legislatures responding to grass roots fears or public hysteria.

I want to extend my point one step further. The problems of universities, as they attempt to protect their scientific research from adversary attacks generated by well-organized community groups playing on the fears of the general public, are a rather faithful reflection of the problems of the nation as a whole addressing major public questions which turn on subtle scientific or technical judgments. America is rapidly exhausting its supplies of petroleum as our consumption of oil and natural gas continues to increase under the demands of our standard of living. By 1990 our dependence on Middle East production should be virtually complete. We can expect to be in the same position as the Japanese are now, and indeed competing with the Japanese as well as other industrial nations for scarce oil. Even today more than half our consumption derives from sources outside the United States. Yet many intelligent people still believe that the oil embargo was contrived in order to produce profits for American oil companies. It is almost shocking to discover that half the country still does not believe that we import oil.

To what extent is this astonishing level of misunderstanding and misinformation a reflection of the adversary character of our public life as we attempt to develop an effective energy policy? If a large number of elected state Attorneys General see the oil companies as conspirators, what is the general public to believe? Adversary struggle, claim and counterclaim, blizzards of publicity from public officials and public interest groups seeking divestiture legislation, will not produce new oil. Our people are being encouraged to believe that it is all a plot, that nuclear energy is dangerous to life, and that solar energy development is being blocked by monied interests trying to profit from the oil crisis. As far as I can judge from what I know of the facts nearly all of this is the purest form of nonsense. No competent scientist, oil expert or solar energy engineer believes that this adversary rhetoric is solving any of our problems or doing the nation any good.

The idea that the adversary legal and political struggle characterizing the environmental protection movement in America during the last decade may be doing great damage to our scientific and technological capability is bound to be a very unpopular one but I fear that it is uncomfortably close to the mark. And the basic question persists. How are we to find more responsible ways to make sound public judgments on critical national issues such as the control of energy, science, and technology?

First I believe that we must be extremely careful to avoid legislating American science out of existence under the guise of environmental protection. Legislators must exercise forbearance in responding to the undifferentiated fears of the general public. They should be willing to ask for the help and advice of the best people in the scientific community in establishing the trade-offs between environmental protection and modern technology.

Second, local authorities should be extremely reluctant to intervene in the administration of research at universities when legal actions are brought by community advocates claiming public safety violations or environmental damage. The necessary controls can and indeed must be established at the national level under the guidance of scientifically competent agencies such as the National Academy of Science or the National Institutes of Health. Local intervention in the form now developing in Boston and New York City will only produce chaos. It has the potential for driving scientific research out of the northeast region of the country with all the economic danger to our area that will follow from such irrationality.

Finally, the government and the bench should turn more frequently to special commissions constituted from the best and most responsible members of the scientific community in an effort to formulate wise public policy on the protection of the environment, public health, and on all major public safety questions. I have heard of proposals that a "science court" be established for the resolution of disputes in these technically demanding areas, but I oppose the concept because it introduces courtroom advocacy into a branch of knowledge where advocacy and overstatement becloud issues instead of illuminating them. Prestigious commissions with high credibility have rendered great service toward the solution of subtle public questions in Britain. We ought to make more use of the idea in this country as an effective healing force and as an alternative to overzealous advocacy. The issues are far too complex and too much is at stake to permit us to destroy our scientific leadership in a welter of adversary struggles with narrow constituency interests. Such struggles are clearly avoidable if there is a national will to do so.

And so here we are five hundred years after the birth of Saint Thomas More still trying to harmonize the law with justice, still striving for utopia. The English system of law managed to survive the caprices of Henry VIII becoming eventually the cornerstone in which America's great legal traditions were built. For more than two centuries we and our English colleagues have shown the rest of the world how societies can govern themselves through the application of principles rather than through the raw exercise of authority. Our legal structure is not perfect. It is natural to dwell on its imperfections and to consider what remains to be done as I have done this evening. But that effort should not divert us from recognizing what Saint Thomas More sought when he demanded adherence to a principle from a monarch who viewed his merest whim as the essence of law. The principles of Anglo-American law continue to illuminate our lives and to guide our destinies five centuries later. It is perhaps the finest contribution to humanism that man has yet devised and we must continue to seek its perfection.

FEDERAL SUPPORT OF SCIENCE AND MEDICINE[3]

JOSEPH A. CALIFANO, JR.[4]

One of the more active cabinet members of the Carter Administration is Joseph A. Califano, Jr., Secretary of Health, Education, and Welfare. In 1977, he gave thirty-one speeches, testified frequently before congressional committees, and held frequent press conferences. He has been "the fulcrum of every major domestic policy issue" including welfare, busing, abortion, social security, treatment of the handicapped, student aid, smoking, health costs, saccharin, government reorganization, urban policy, and the federal drug law (David E. Rosenbaum, New York *Times,* March 19, 1978).

On Sunday, December 18, 1977, Secretary Califano delivered the principal address at the winter commencement of the University of Michigan, Ann Arbor. He spoke to the 1,800 graduates and their parents, relatives, and friends who filled every seat of great Hill Auditorium (Detroit *News,* December 19, 1977).

As in his other talks, he turned his attention to the general policy issues facing his department. One of his assistants reported, "Although he works with a speech writer . . . he puts a great deal of his own creativity and energy into the preparation of his speeches" (letter from Jolin M. Blamphin, Media Relations Division, Department of Health, Education, and Welfare, April 18, 1978).

The fact that the University of Michigan was planning to do research in recombinant DNA (deoxyribonucleic acid) formed the background for his talk. The university had received $235,000 to finance the redesign of laboratories for the safe handling of hazardous material. Nevertheless, many persons in the community questioned the wisdom of this type of research. Sensing their mood, Califano said:

> It was the crime of Prometheus—or his achievement—to steal fire from the gods. We twentieth century humans

[3] Delivered at the winter commencement, University of Michigan, Ann Arbor, at 1:45 P.M., Sunday, December 18, 1977. Title supplied by editor. Quoted by permission.

[4] For biographical note, see Appendix.

> have outdistanced Prometheus: We have stolen from the gods not only fire, but the atom and the secrets of the living cell.
>
> It was the fate of Prometheus to be chained to a rock for his impertinence. It is our fate, in our age, to be chained to the new problems we create by our cleverness.

He knew that, as HEW secretary, he had to respond to the controversy involving government support of such programs as DNA research, abortion, and other medical and scientific projects.

In contrast to President McGill of Columbia University, Califano called for open debate on the issues of recombinant DNA research and government financing of abortion and sterilization, the war against cancer, and organ transplants. In his solution to the problem of what kind of research the government should engage in, he encouraged further discussion and investigations by the citizenry, saying, "Today, more than ever, democracy depends on an informed and engaged citizenry. I urge you to be both—informed and engaged. Information without engagement is the stuff of political impotence in modern day America: engagement without information is the stuff of demagoguery."

Because it was known that Califano opposed federal financial support for poor women seeking abortion, the National Organization for Women (NOW) had organized a protest. Thus, when the secretary finished speaking, about fifty persons in the audience turned their backs on him. "In the same way he has turned his back on the poor women of America, we ask the students to turn their backs on him," said Mary Dence, president of the Ann Arbor NOW chapter (Detroit *News,* December 19, 1977).

I am grateful for your hospitality—and delighted and honored that I have received, in only a few minutes, what has taken you years to achieve: a degree from the University of Michigan. If the record of past Michigan alumni is any guide, my future is now assured.

It may not have been your first purpose, Dr. Fleming. But by awarding this honorary degree, you have done more than honor the recipient; you have created one more enthusiastic rooter for Michigan's Rose Bowl team.

It is a treat to see my old friend and predecessor, Dean Wilbur Cohen. I find it especially encouraging to see a former Secretary of Health, Education, and Welfare not only alive—but healthy, happy, and gainfully employed.

Last week, Wilbur Cohen sent me a recent edition of the Michigan *Daily*. In it, a student writer had this advice about my remarks today: "Considering the job market, . . . perhaps a message with some practical value would be in order, like, say, 'welfare and the recent college graduate.' "

I have decided not to follow that suggestion. I have abundant faith in your talent and resourcefulness.

Nor do I come with gifts of wisdom or advice, or a set of modern-day commandments for our exciting and perplexing world.

I come instead with questions—some ultimate questions—to which I hope you will turn your fresh minds no matter what your career. They are questions of ethics and morality that have been infinitely complicated in recent years by politics and finances. They are questions literally of life and death. They deserve—and will probably command—your attention for the rest of your lives.

The University of Michigan is an especially appropriate forum at which to raise these issues. At this great center of research and learning, frontiers of knowledge are touched every day—and often pushed back.

Last year, the university conducted some $75 million of research—much of it basic in a very real sense. Almost three-quarters of that $75 million comes from the federal government.

We begin with an ancient question—revived with electric urgency: How can we cope with the ethical and moral problems that exploding knowledge brings?

It is a universal assumption among scientists, and a popular assumption among Americans generally, that all knowledge is good. But at least since the dawn of the nuclear age, we have been confronted with the uncomfortable reality that knowledge can be put to use in ways that are not necessarily benign—indeed, in ways that may threaten the survival of mankind.

In the past few years, breakthroughs in biological research have stirred the kind of fears that were aroused by the revolution in physics a generation ago: The fears that our scientists in their laboratories might be re-enacting the myth of Pandora's Box—that by their relentless exploration of the unexplored, they might, however unintentionally, unleash upon humanity forces of frightening potential.

At the far frontiers of biological research, scientists long ago found ways to create new molecules; now they have found ways to alter genes. Their efforts hold out hope that we may cure some intractable diseases—but their efforts also raise the specter that we could inadvertently create new forms of life that threaten the environment, or even our lives. Dare we seek the gains from this research, while ignoring its potential risks? And if the answer is, as I think it must be, to conduct such research but to regulate it—how do we strike a proper balance between reasonable and necessary restraint and unwarranted fettering of free inquiry?

The technology of medicine has moved into the awe-inspiring era of vital-organ transplants. Some organs for those transplants, as you know, must be taken from dead or dying patients. This technology raises stunning questions that are intellectually and morally confounding: When does death actually occur? Whose business is it to define death? Should each individual, or should society, have the right to specify when life shall no longer be sustained by extraordinary technology?

These questions of knowledge and its consequences are complex enough. But they are made even more difficult by a relatively recent historic development: The entrance of big government, with its massive power and giant budgets, into fields of science and medicine which once were local and private.

In other generations, for example, health was a matter between a patient and a doctor with a little black bag. Health research was conducted in small laboratories and financed by individuals or medical schools. Our citizens had no trouble distinguishing between exaggerated Hollywood versions of Madame Curie and Dr. Frankenstein.

But today, health care is the third biggest business in America. Twelve cents of every federal tax dollar is paid to the health industry. About ninety percent of the biomedical research in this nation is financed by the national government. With the arrival of expensive and exotic psychosurgery, heart transplants, heart pumps, kidney dialysis, artificial hip joints, microscopic surgery, and jolting electric shock to revive a stilled heart, government's direct involvement in some of our most difficult and controversial scientific problems has markedly increased. And our citizens are confused and believe the once sharp images of Madame Curie and Dr. Frankenstein have become somewhat blurred.

This deep involvement of government inevitably thrusts into the arena of politics and public policy a tangled mass of ethical and moral questions—with discomforting consequences for those of us who govern.

If government supports heart-transplant research, can government escape the question of when death actually occurs?

If government finances health care, then government becomes the center of bitter controversies about what it shall finance: abortion and sterilization, for example.

When does life begin? When does death occur?

In another age, these two most profound of questions would have been fodder for Talmudic scholars, Jesuit priests, and family doctors listening for a heartbeat.

But the peculiar and inescapable fact of our age is that these questions are intensely political and highly scientific as well.

It is a disquieting characteristic of our time that government cannot escape such sensitive and controversial questions. There is no neutral ground on which government can comfortably and securely stand—for just as no decision is a decision, so too is neutrality. Any decision by government on the financing of some, all or no abortions, for example, will distress large numbers of earnest, sincere, and humane people.

The entrance of government into the arena of moral and ethical decision-making is complicated by the blunt reality of limited resources.

In an era of finite budgets, how do we choose what to distribute to whom—when what we choose may result in life for some and death for others?

The geniuses of modern medicine and bioengineering may some day perfect for us a workable, artificial heart. But do we have the geniuses to decide who should be eligible to have such a marvelous, life-sustaining and expensive device?

All of us support the battle against cancer. But how shall we deploy our limited troops in that battle? What proportion of our budgets should we spend on basic research, to help future generations escape the dread disease? And what proportion should we devote to expensive long-shot therapies for those who now have the disease? Who determines this delicate balance and how?

The artificial heart that I mentioned earlier is for tomorrow, if at all. But kidney dialysis machines are here today. A nationwide hemodialysis program helps maintain fifty thousand patients at a cost approaching one billion dollars a year, a cost borne almost entirely by the federal government.

Thus the nation has taken responsibility for the complete care of victims of this one catastrophic illness. But what about other victims of other illnesses? To what extent do they have a claim on limited public funds? Their lives are also at stake. By what calculus of justice or mercy shall governments decide whose life shall be saved and whose lost.

If you wonder what a Secretary of Health, Education, and Welfare thinks about, now you have some idea: He thinks about questions like these. And if he chances to look out his office window, he may see a crowd of demonstrators expressing their strong feelings on one of these questions—or several of them. HEW is the only department of government in which both motherhood and apple pie are controversial.

Questions people once sought to have answered by prayer, issues once left for scientists to resolve in their laboratories are now debated on the floor of Congress, or thrown into the HEW regulatory process.

Consider a random sampling of issues we face today—or have faced in recent weeks at HEW:

What are the proper limits on fetal research? Under what circumstances should the national government finance abortion? Under what circumstances should we release potentially life-saving but potentially fatal drugs? To what extent should we fund psychosurgery that alters the mind? Should we spend new federal money on expensive medical technology or on providing basic health care to the poor? To what extent should we hold people responsible for taking care of their own health before the government begins paying their medical bills?

And what about federal financing of sterilization? We may agree that informed consent by the patient is a necessary ingredient in a decision to be sterilized. But how do we define informed consent? Is it possible, for example, for a minor to give informed consent? What about a retarded or mentally incompetent adult—or child? Can anyone—even the spouse or parents—provide informed consent? Is there any such thing as informed consent by a young man or young woman to an irreversible procedure like sterilization that goes to the marrow of the human condition?

All these are questions that concern not just physicians, scholars, researchers, and government officials. They concern all of us. In a democracy, we wisely hold that such questions are too important to be left to mere experts.

Certainly these are not questions for one department of government—or even for the courts or Congress alone. They are questions for society—which is to say, for you and me. The experts can give us a wealth of technical information upon which to base our judgments—but in matters of morals and other social values, mere information is not enough.

Science has become too important to be left to scientists and government has always been too important to be left to the governors.

All great power—whether the power of knowledge, the power of government, or the power of wealth—can be dangerous unless it is accompanied by great wisdom. There is no individual man or woman wise enough to answer the questions I have raised. What we must do is establish institutions and processes that will draw together our best wisdom, from all possible sources, to temper knowledge and to guide government.

A pluralistic society, facing such intrinsically complex questions, will never find a single right answer that will satisfy all its citizens. But there are some basic tenets of decision-making we should follow:

First, we can assure due process. If we cannot guarantee right decisions, we can guarantee that we decide in the right way. This means decisions made democratically, through wide consultation, not by special elites. Indeed, in a diverse, contentious nation whose people seldom achieve unanimous agreement, the process by which we reach decisions becomes as important as the decisions we make. We cannot assure that everyone will agree on a controversial issue like recombinant DNA research. But we can at least assure that everyone has been heard. This is the slowest way, the most inconvenient way—but in a democracy, the only way to make such decisions.

Second, we can wrestle with these questions in the open. The whole society cannot, perhaps, participate in highly technical decisions about mass immunization programs for influenza in which the vaccine that saves millions may kill a few. But it can witness such decisions and it must. When the stakes are so high, when profound values are in conflict and raw emotions are laid bare, the temptation can be irresistible for leaders, whether doctors or researchers or government bureaucrats, to seek security and calm behind closed doors. But in today's world, the rooms behind closed doors offer no safety—only the illusion of safety.

Decision-makers in science and medicine must learn the hard lesson that politicians have absorbed in recent years: closed doors breed distrust—even if what happens behind those doors is perfectly legitimate. Perhaps our people cannot share in making every big decision; but they should at least see them made and bear witness to them.

Decisions made in the sunshine are particularly important when so many difficult questions are being decided in the executive branch of national government, outside the processes of congressional debate, without sufficient political debate in county seats, city councils, and state legislatures.

Third, we should resist the temptation to give glib answers to unanswerable questions.

It is tempting particularly to bureaucrats writing laws and regulations and to scientists, whose business is solving problems, to leave no question unanswered.

Yet we must recognize that in a free, pluralistic society there are some questions which have no single ready answer. On such questions, it is important, I think, to go slow, to count to ten. We should hope for moderate progress toward consensus, rather than press impatiently for immediate national solutions. This may mean leaving some difficult questions to be answered in different ways by different communities for some time. But quick national answers to deep questions of values and morals are usually imposed from above without sufficient attention to unintended consequences—and so they solve little and generate great strife.

We should trust our pluralistic system to do its work from the bottom up. However frustrated and impatient we may become with it, it is the system by which consensus is built on searing issues. Winston Churchill was right when he said that democracy is the worst form of government—except for all others.

Fourth and finally, the institutions we create to help

make the difficult technical, political, and moral choices posed by expanding scientific knowledge and limited resources, must be broadly-based. Whether they be hospital ethics committees, peer review boards, biohazard councils or national or presidential advisory committees—the institutions we choose to wrestle with these questions should represent us all, all the varied beliefs and values that compete in America. These institutions must reach out for all views to be inclusive, not, and I use this word in both its senses, exclusive.

Otherwise, our decisions are likely to reflect not consensus, but bias.

It was the crime of Prometheus—or his achievement—to steal fire from the gods. We twentieth century humans have outdistanced Prometheus: We have stolen from the gods not only fire, but the atom and the secrets of the living cell.

It was the fate of Prometheus to be chained to a rock for his impertinence. It is our fate, in our age, to be chained to the new problems we create by our cleverness.

I have raised many questions to which I offer no certain answers. I submit to you that even a Solomon, Aquinas or Hippocrates would meet his match if faced with these questions in the last quarter of the twentieth century.

Moreover, we have chosen in this nation to be suspicious of individual wisdom as applied to the body politic. Indeed an essential ingredient of pluralistic democracy is to test such wisdom skeptically and openly.

Today, more than ever, democracy depends on an informed and engaged citizenry. I urge you to be both—informed and engaged. Information without engagement is the stuff of political impotence in modern day America; engagement without information is the stuff of demagoguery.

You can ignore the questions I have raised—and scores of others like them—only at your peril and your nation's. The relentless pursuit of knowledge and truth will continue —as it should. The involvement of government in that pursuit will deepen. The limitations of our resources will become more pronounced.

The issues these three inexorable facts raise are too important for someone else. They deserve your personal attention.

Whatever career you pursue, I hope you will give them that attention. And, if you do, I cannot promise you will find clear and hard answers. I can promise that you will enrich yourselves and your generation, that you will be exhilarated by the excitement of informed engagement, and that you will share the satisfaction of having, each in your own individual way, made this society a little better place for yourself and the rest of us.

AN INFORMED SOCIETY: COMPLEXITIES AND CHALLENGES

THE FAILURE OF SCIENTISTS TO COMMUNICATE[1]

TRENT C. ROOT, JR.[2]

Trent C. Root, vice president for corporate relations of the Texas Utilities Company (Dallas) spoke at one of the sessions of the International Conference on Energy Use at the Convention Center, Tucson, Arizona, on October 25, 1977. This meeting brought together, from many countries of the world, representatives of universities, power companies, trade associations, agricultural cooperatives, and related businesses and industries. Architects, government officials, university professors, scientists, engineers, public relations specialists, industrialists, and business people were among those who attended. The planners outlined the motivating force behind the twelve sessions as follows: "The prospect of diminishing fossil fuel supplies and progressive degradation of the environment have focused world attention on energy needs and use. It has become increasingly obvious that we must examine our energy use patterns in order to improve efficiency and curtail waste."

A session was devoted to "public communication" because the planners recognized the fact that "scientists and engineers do not adequately communicate with the general public" (letter from Jon B. Riffel) and consequently that technical and scientific advances can move no faster or further than the general public is willing to accept and to accommodate them (see speech by William J. McGill, above). Root brought this problem into sharp focus in his conclusion:

> Nowhere is there a greater need for the presence of the scientist today than in the field of energy use—where facts, hard facts, must be emphasized. Nowhere is it more vital for the scientist to become involved than in clarifying issues in energy where wrong decision and wrong action could jeopardize the future of generations.

[1] Delivered at the Marriott Hotel, Tucson, Arizona, 8:30–11:30 A.M., October 25, 1977, at International Conference on Energy Use. Quoted by permission.
[2] For biographical note, see Appendix.

I guess, before we spend the morning telling you our ideas of how to communicate with the public, we should discuss, do you really want to communicate with the public?, and too, whether you want to or not—should you?

In ancient Rome when the favorite pastime was throwing Christians to the lions, a story occurred that reminds me of my subject this morning.

This particular Christian was thrown to a lion. The lion grabbed him by the shoulder, threw him to the ground; and suddenly walked away and went to sleep. The Christian got up rubbing his shoulder and walked back into the cells in the coliseum. The other Christians gathered around and said, "How did you do that?" And he said, "It's simple. I whispered into the lion's ear that 'After the meal, you will be expected to make a few remarks.' "

It's not always fun—it's hard work—this show business of communicating—it's particularly hard for scientists, or doctors, or utility men—or anyone practicing a discipline that has its own language. It's apropos that you have a utility man speaking on this subject. For years we didn't communicate. We had no need. Our service was near perfect—our price was declining. Energy to fuel our generators was plentiful. And if someone did have the audacity to attack us in the press—we simply ignored it—hid our heads in the sand, and it all went away.

And then times changed. Rates started up. The economics of size no longer offset inflation. Fuels became expensive. The housewife saw her light bill going up 10-20-50 even 100 percent. In that atmosphere you can no longer hide your head in the sand. The public (that housewife) demands *and* has the right to know about your business—because it's their business. So we had to learn. It wasn't and isn't easy. Like scientists we have our own language. Let me give you an example.

My Company has constructed a large lignite-fueled power plant in east Texas. Since lignite is a low-Btu content coal and reasonably damp, it takes an enormous boiler to provide steam for a unit of this size: 750,000 kw. The boiler which is about the size of a thirty-story office building also has to have an enormous quantity of oxygen to support the combustion of the lignite; and so has large fans pushing air into the boiler and other large fans pulling the air out of the boiler.

This past summer the large fans pushing the air into the boiler stopped working and the large fans pulling the air out of the boiler caused a vacuum which sucked the walls in about four feet. Since this particular unit has a low fuel cost and it materially affects the billing to our customers, we felt they deserved to know what happened. So we asked the engineers in our generating company to write a News Release. Let me quote that release to you.

NEGATIVE FURNACE EXCURSION
UNIT #1 MLSES
July 21, 1977

At 0216 hours July 21, 1977, a negative furnace excursion occurred on Unit #1. This occurred when two of the four I.D. fans tripped while the unit was at full load.

This boiler automatically goes into a unit run-back condition when this occurs.

The closing of dampers plus the reduction of the furnace fires created a vacuum condition in the boiler which resulted in some tube leaks and slight structural damage.

There were no malfunctions during this incident. These controls responded as they were designed to do.

The unit will be out-of-service between three to four weeks.

So you can see we are still learning to communicate. Needless to say, this News Release was completely rewritten.

Now, how about scientists. Should you learn? Should you communicate? Especially should you communicate about energy supply and use? It's not easy. You may find yourself in a position you don't like or with a reputation you don't like.

In 1975, a dissertation called *The Visible Scientist* was published. It examined the changing relationship between science and society, and the impact that a few scientists—about forty of them in a scientific community of about two million—had on public issues.

Why do only a handful of scientists continually get so much attention from the mass media? How influential are they in forming public opinion? What, if any, characteristics do they share?

Dr. Rae Goodell found that forty men and women comprised the visible scientists.

The top twenty of her list in 1975 were: B. F. Skinner, Margaret Mead, Jonas Salk, Wernher von Braun, Linus Pauling, Paul Ehrlich, Isaac Asimov, Jane Goodall, Albert Sabin, William Shockley, Noam Chomsky, Barry Commoner, James Watson, Edward Teller, Rene Dubos, Glenn Seaborg, Arthur Jensen, Harold Urey, George Wald, and Joshua Lederberg.

In probing more closely, Dr. Goodell discovered that the twenty most visible scientists shared five characteristics in common. I'd like to go over them with you.

One. Each has a current topic. The scientists are issue-oriented. They talk about the ramifications of their research rather than their research. They speak out on areas of general concern, such as the deteriorating environment, population explosion, preventing common colds, and the energy crisis.

When Rene Dubos, the microbiologist and environmentalist, saw the list of well-known scientists, he said, "The list reflects what problems are in the minds of people today."

Paul Ehrlich told Dr. Goodell during their interview: "My visibility was partly the result of having my mouth open at that particular point in time when apparently people were ripe to listen to population problems."

As issues change, so do the visible scientists. Thus, Ehrlich is no longer as much in the public eye today, with interest in population problems having receded. Margaret Mead, who has moved from one issue to another along with shifts in public interest, is as well-known today as in 1975.

Two. Each is controversial. Visible scientists are not very popular in the scientific community. They speak out from personal conscience rather than from popular consensus. When Linus Pauling came out in favor of Vitamin C as a sound treatment for the common cold, he invited the wrath of the entire medical community, which had opposed megavitamin treatment for generations. He got the expected reaction, including the accusation, that being over seventy, he was senile. The visible scientist looks for new approaches, and finding them, advocates change. His position is usually interesting and debatable—not frightening nor absurd.

Three. Each is articulate. They abandon their scientific jargon to speak in a language the general public can understand. They are at ease with newspeople. Part of Margaret Mead's appeal to journalists, for instance, is her ability to make statements devoid of disclaimers and qualifiers such as "possibly," "one solution I might suggest," "the evidence tends to point to," or "my opinion on that would be." Adding to their quotability is their adroit use of imagery, indeed one of most valuable tools in explaining complex material to the public.

Fourth. Each has a colorful image. With competition for news space extremely intense, the scientist who has a colorful accent, an idiosyncratic style of dress, an engaging manner, is likely to be sought after. Dr. Goodell dissects charisma in the following manner: "Rene Dubos has a grandfatherly charm (he is seventy-three) and an expressive French accent (he emigrated in 1924) which is reminiscent of Maurice Chevalier. William Shockley shows signs of paranoia, about the press, blacks, critics. Linus Pauling is a political radical. Paul Ehrlich has had a vasectomy." While most of the popular scientists seem to possess a natural flair, others encourage the colorful image or work at it.

Fifth. Each has established a credible reputation. Science reporters and editors are wary of stories that arise from an unfamiliar source. If they are not familiar with the scientist, they check with other scientists. If a scientist is not known, he can get attention from the media by being associated with a widely-known institution. The chances are, reporters figure, that if he has been hired by Bell Laboratories or Harvard University, he is reputable and safe. Thus many stories about unknown scientists often begin: "A Stanford University biologist announced today . . ." The ultimate in a personal, checkable credential is the Nobel Prize, of course.

Ladies and gentlemen, perhaps none of us here today has ever qualified for the roster of the twenty most visible scientists. Perhaps most of us would not want the headaches associated with getting on such a roster, headaches such as separation from our basic scientific work, the suspicion of our colleagues, the risks of having our statements sensationalized. The hard work that goes along with communicating. But I doubt that there is anyone here today who would not welcome the opportunity to learn how to communicate with the public better. I doubt that there is anyone here who hasn't felt the urgency of having to communicate technical facts to a non-technical audience in a language that can both inform *and* persuade.

And whether you like it or not, the need for communicating effectively is growing more intense each day as we delve deeper into energy issues, unearthing more and more problems associated with energy use and diminishing supplies.

The public will support energy programs to the extent that it understands the issues involved in those programs. It will reject those programs out of hand if it has no comprehension of the issues involved.

For example, in June of this year, a Harris poll found that those who were best informed about oil import needs in this country were the most receptive to our President Carter's call for energy conservation and sacrifice. Of those who felt the President called for too many sacrifices on the part of the public, forty-one percent thought we had enough oil—in other words, did not believe we have a developing worldwide energy crisis.

Even today, a large segment of the American public behaves as if there were no energy crisis. Gasoline consumption set records last summer. Use of electricity has been at an all-time high. Consumption so far this year is more than seven percent above that of a year ago. And even today, only forty-eight percent of the public knows that we must import oil to meet our energy needs. I'm sure the same situations exist in other countries.

Obviously, scientists have to speak up, and to speak up more clearly if we are all going to make any progress towards securing our energy future.

The surprising thing about this so-called energy debate is that the voices least often heard are the very voices that could dispel much of the confusion and the controversy through the introduction of massive doses of fact. As government bureaucrats, educators, public interest group lobbyists, and businessmen join what is amounting to an energy fray, the one figure that has stayed out of the arena—the figure that *should be there*—is the scientist.

There are exceptions, of course, notably in the area of nuclear power. But for the most part, the scientist has maintained an aloof silence in the face of the energy crisis, a silence that is not only unwarranted but wasteful considering that the scientist's statements on energy would probably be accepted ahead of everyone else's.

I will cite only two examples of the public's high regard for science and scientists.

In June of last year, Californians debated a referendum on nuclear power called Proposition 15. If you said YES to the proposition you said NO to nuclear power. At the beginning of the debate, the NO's waged a losing battle. In three months, however, they turned the campaign around and were ultimately successful in convincing Californians that a ban on nuclear power was not in their best interests. Proposition 15 was defeated.

In this debate, scientists and scientific organizations clearly showed themselves to be the most effective spokesmen on the nuclear issue in California.

A striking feature of a survey taken at that time showed that the usefulness of the scientist was not dependent on his personal qualifications.

One of the opinion research companies studying public opinion during the referendum asked respondents this question:

> I'm going to read you the names of some people and groups who have taken a public position on Proposition 15. After each name, could you tell me whether their opinion on the nuclear initiative would make you more inclined or less inclined to support their position?

The list included politicians, environmentalists, entertainment figures, and scientists. Scientists scored high in public credibility. In fact, the list included the names of two fictitious scientists, Floyd Snow and Donald Pettit whose names were drawn from the telephone book but who were identified as scientists. The public said the opinion of the two would make them more likely to support their position.

And recently, when the public was asked to rate what it thought makes this country great and will keep it great over the next ten years, the public chose "industrial and scientific knowhow" from a list of twenty-five factors, ahead of such assets as rich natural resources, a hard-working people, military strength, or living under a system of guaranteed individual freedoms.

But while the job of communicating with the public is easy because of the public's high regard for scientists, it is also difficult because of the public's general lack of science literacy. This is not to be critical, but it is simply to state the facts, which in the words of Richard Atkinson, head of the National Science Foundation, are these: "There is a basic incomprehension of what science is all about, how it works, and what the principles of the basic sciences are."

This lack of science background is particularly unfortunate when it comes to energy issues, where the public seems to be laboring under the mistaken notion that a scientific breakthrough on energy will preserve their lifestyles. "There is no five year solution to our energy problems," says Atkinson. "Science just doesn't operate with those turnaround times."

In his view, the sorry state of science literacy can be traced partly to the schools, which with the advent of Sputnik and the Space Age, introduced a lot of high powered curricula that resulted in tough courses and "fewer and fewer students learning more and more."

Atkinson suggested that liberal education include a solid grounding in basic sciences so that citizens would be able to understand more clearly what is at stake in issues such as the fate of nuclear breeder reactors and research into the gene manufacturing possibilities of recombinant DNA. "Most people don't have the vaguest notion of what those are all about," he added, "and the level of debate could be a lot higher."

There are other obstacles to communicating with the public effectively on science. To cite a few of the most obvious: Government bureaucracy and a value system on the part of politicians that frequently limits their thinking to the next election rather than to the long-range future of the planet. A press without enough science specialists to handle complex scientific stories competently. Corporate machineries that tend to rob scientists of their independence, sometimes compelling them to remain silent about an unethical or potentially hazardous design or practice. Lastly, the scientist himself, who, committed as he is to the pursuit of the knowledge and truth of his craft, tends to seek out those who can enhance that knowledge namely, other scientists—and to avoid the uninitiated, who can't. Many scientists are unwilling to explore the avenues of communicating with the public because it is time consuming. It takes time away from basic research and other scientific responsibilities.

But the truth is, we're all running out of time on energy. A colleague of mine, the executive of a utility, once told his audience that the reason they weren't communicating well with one another is because they were on different timetables. He said:

> One reason why so many still yawn at reports of an energy crisis is that our watches may be said to keep different time.
>
> In the electric utility business, for example, it is already 1985.
>
> The reason we have adequate power—in this room, for instance, where the lights are on and it is cool—lies in decisions made and money committed five and ten years ago. It's all a question of lead times, of having to act now so as to bring about desired results ten years down the road.

The time to speak up about the facts of our energy problem is now. The way to do it is clearly, with concern for the vast effects, today's energy policies are going to have on our lives, and the lives of our children.

I think that in telling the energy story, we will find the press a willing listener. The press is eager to hear from scientists in government, industry or education with a relevant story to tell, and who know how to tell it.

In closing, let me just share with you what I believe is the most important thing the scientist should keep in mind when communicating with the public. And that's this: The public is asking that scientists, many of whose disciplines were once regarded as detached intellectual activities, clarify the facts on socially-relevant issues. The public is asking scientists to communicate in readily understandable language. The public is asking scientists to direct their efforts to problems that taxpayers, rather than the theoretical physicists, are interested in solving. In fact, the public is asking a great deal of scientists because it's asking scientists to transcend the dimensions of science itself.

I think the public is right to be asking these things of you. I think when you give it your full consideration, you will agree.

Nowhere is there a greater need for the presence of the scientist today than in the field of energy use—where facts, hard facts, must be emphasized. Nowhere is it more vital for the scientist to become involved than in clarifying issues in energy where wrong decision and wrong action could jeopardize the future of generations. If science fails in this mission, history itself may fail.

YES, you should communicate. Hopefully, this morning you will learn additional things that will help you in that communication chore.

BUSINESS'S RESPONSIBILITY IN AN INFORMATION SOCIETY [3]

HAROLD W. MCGRAW, JR.[4]

The phenomenal increase in knowledge, the complexity of modern enterprise, the magnitude of decisions, and the rapidity of communication have precipitated what Harold McGraw, Jr., president of McGraw-Hill, Inc., called an "information revolution." To function effectively the decision-maker must seek a means to store, index, and retrieve information rapidly. This subject, the efficient handling of information, was pursued at the forty-sixth international conference of the Financial Executives Institute, meeting at the Washington Hilton, Washington, D.C., on October 17, 1977. The institute has an international membership of 9,500, representing 5,500 companies, and the audience at the meeting was made up of the financial officers of top corporations throughout the world.

The speaker for this occasion was Harold W. McGraw, Jr., chairman, president, and chief executive officer of McGraw-Hill, Inc. His speech set forth the dimensions and complexities of "the information business," and reviewed the roles of the US Postal Service, the telephone system, and private-sector information companies. McGraw pointed out the difficulties in the regulation of this phase of modern life and the enormous amount of wisdom necessary to regulate and control it. Stressing the importance of the problem, he said, "I believe very deeply that the control and management of information will become the major component of power in American society. Effective access to an efficient information system will be indispensable to any business enterprise and indeed to any of the educational, governmental or other enterprises of our society."

Those interested in organizational communication will find this speech particularly enlightening.

Today, I would like to share with you my concern about an emerging problem which is only now beginning to be

[3] Delivered at forty-sixth International Conference of the Financial Executives Institute, Washington Hilton Hotel, October 17, 1977. Quoted by permission.

[4] For biographical note, see Appendix.

recognized as a critical national issue. The problem is a product of today's information revolution, and it is already having a real impact on every corporation in America. It is a matter of concern not only for the information business but also for each of you, regardless of what kind of business you're in.

Because I *am* in the information business, the dimensions of the problem are perhaps becoming more apparent. I only wish the solutions were equally clear. I can't bring you answers today, but I do hope to heighten your awareness of the problem and to enlist *your* assistance in working toward solutions.

It's only natural that I turn to a group such as yours with this message. Financial executives have a responsibility to analyze and report the past, to help control the present, to anticipate and budget for the future. The handling of information is at the center of all these responsibilities. The ability to create and to collect financial and operating data, to analyze and interpret it, to report it, and to make decisions based on it is what your job is all about.

I do not have to tell you how dependent American business has become on the efficient handling of information. In part this is due to every company's increasing need for information about its own operations. And as corporate enterprises have become larger, more complex, more far flung geographically, their effective management requires a more and more extensive flow of carefully analyzed information.

That's *internal* information. But the need for external information is equally important. Sensitive *and timely* awareness of changes in tastes, markets, resources, government regulations, economic trends, and competitors' strategies can make possible the success of any enterprise. And a failure to achieve that awareness can determine its failure.

Nor do I have to describe the electronic miracles that have revolutionized the handling of data and helped us to meet those information needs—the computers, the satellites, the data communications equipment, the terminals, the chips the size of a fingernail that can now contain and manipulate data that would have required a roomful of vacuum tubes and relays twenty years ago. And more technological miracles are under way.

This meeting of information needs and advanced information technology has produced a true revolution. Unfortunately, that revolution has had to take place within a framework of laws, regulations, and governmental policy dating to a past generation. The Federal Communications Act goes back to 1934, before television or the computer or the satellite. Until January 1, we will still live under a copyright law passed in 1909—and even the new law makes no effort to deal with the computer.

Bringing our mass of law, regulation, and policy into accord with the technological and operational needs of this new information society is a complex job which is going on right now, all around us. It is taking place in court cases, in Federal Communications Commission proceedings, in Congressional committee hearings, in executive branch actions, in the decisions of private corporations. As a result, some of the decisions are contradictory; most are made without coordination. They are taken too often with little overall sense of purpose or direction and, most unfortunately, with very little interaction with the business community as a whole. By and large, the only companies which have risen to speak their minds have been the information companies themselves, such as the broadcasting networks and Ma Bell—each with its own special interests to protect. What we urgently need is the point of view of business in general, of executives like yourselves, who may not be in the information business, but who depend on that business for the vital daily needs of their own companies.

Out of the dozens that could be listed, there are just three problems, or groups of problems, I want to discuss with you this morning:

One is what sort of basic structure of communication—for example, postal and telephone services—are we going to have in the United States.

The *second* is what the policies of the federal government will be with regard to the availability and dissemination of its own enormous stores of information.

The *third* is the role of private-sector information companies, and the relation of government regulation and government competition to the ability of those companies to serve the public.

Let's look first at the Postal Service and the telephone system. Each has served us well. Both now must adjust to new technologies that may reinforce or may make heavy inroads into the partial monopolies they have enjoyed. Governmental policy decisions will determine how they relate to those new technologies.

For a long time the Postal Service had a near monopoly of intercity transportation of messages, publications, and parcels. As long-distance telephone service became cheaper and cheaper, it has taken over much of the personal and business communication that once would have gone by first-class mail. One result is that today the principal use of first-class mail relates to money—invoices, statements, bills, checks, the stuff of your functions.

Meanwhile the Postal Service is required to offer a universal service reaching into the smallest village and the most remote home. Competitive enterprises, by confining themselves to the more profitable routes and types of material, can offer that limited service more efficiently and economically than the Postal Service.

The Postal Service is now under a mandate to break even, relying on user charges with the minimal possible subsidy. It has responded to this mandate by cutting service and sharply raising rates. The predictable result is the diversion of more of the second-, third-, and fourth-class mail, to private carriers. The development of electronic funds transfer services may make further deep inroads into the most profitable business the Postal Service has—first-class financial mail—and may create a real crisis indeed. Cutting service and raising rates is a self-defeating policy. Its only outcome can be a bankrupt and collapsing Postal Service.

It is obvious we face critical decisions about its future. An efficient Postal Service remains an absolute necessity for business as well as for American society. Our present policy is not giving it to us. I think we have to face the fact that a totally or nearly totally user-supported Postal Service is a mirage. We must recognize that the social values of a universal service carrying the widest range of materials to every corner of the country is going to have to be sustained by adequate public support.

The telephone system, like the Postal Service, is facing the problem of maintaining a universal, or nearly universal, service while meeting the competition of special services over high-density routes. Once the telephone system was concerned only with conventional voice transmission.

But now we have the need for a wide variety of high-density computer-based data transmission services. Those services cannot be provided independently of the telephone network because of the need to use the network's facilities to distribute messages to individual recipients.

The basic policy question is whether this enormous and increasingly indispensable new area of service will be the exclusive responsibility of the present telephone system or whether other carriers and producers of equipment will have a major role. The consistent policy of the FCC in recent years has been to encourage competition.

The Bell system has objected vigorously, claiming that connection with non-Bell equipment for specialized intercity data transmission services threatens the technical degradation of service, and that selective competition confined to high-density operations and routes will force it to raise rates on the less profitable low-density and residential services. On a broader basis, AT&T has contended that a single overall direction is necessary to create a balanced, technically compatible, well-planned total telephonic communications system.

Independent carriers and producers, however, strongly assert that only the entry of a variety of competitors into the data communications field can assure American society, and especially the business community, of the flexibility and diversity of service and the innovative equipment and techniques that our new world of information will require.

These issues are now being fought out before Congress and in the courts in antitrust actions as well as before the FCC. I feel sure that we must both protect the integrity of the telephone system and also build up a variety of special services. It will take wisdom to reconcile these needs—wisdom in Congress, in the FCC, and in the executive branch offices concerned with telecommunications policy. And it will take a thorough understanding of the business community's needs for efficient, high-quality, specialized data communications services. It is executives like yourselves who best understand and can communicate those needs.

There is a common denominator in the decisions we must make in regard to our basic communications networks. How can we make maximum use of all available contributions to efficient information handling while preserving the strength and integrity of our basic systems? The resultant balanced total system will have to serve the needs of American society generally—government, the educational system, the individual consumer as well as business. Government, education, and consumer organizations have been analyzing and defining their needs and pressing them vigorously on Congress, the administration, and regulatory agencies. Business users have been far less active in pressing and defining their needs.

In many ways, the set of policy issues in the information field with the greatest importance to the business community is the set of policies relating not to the government's role as rule maker and umpire of the information game, but rather to its role as the principal player in that game.

The federal government is by far the largest creator, collector, and consumer of information in the country. In many fields, such as nuclear energy, foreign relations, space exploration, and national security matters, the government indeed is the indispensable original source of information. In addition, as you well know from the endless hours your staffs spend in preparing reports for government agencies, the federal government is *the* great collector of data of our time. In its files are collected literally hundreds of billions of facts about every aspect of the American economy.

We have a dual problem. Access to this enormous treasury of information is essential to the intelligent conduct of our business affairs. Every business firm needs to know swiftly of new or impending laws, regulations, and policies. It needs access to the vast body of information collected by the government.

At the same time, much of the material in government files—tax returns, investigative reports, confidential data submitted by business firms—is essentially private. Its revelation by government could be destructive of the rights of individuals and seriously damaging to corporations through the exposure to competitors of confidential proprietary information.

The Freedom of Information Act and privacy legislation are obviously in tension. But I think the fundamental policy lines are reasonably clear. Except for certain obvious confidential matters, records of the government's own conduct of affairs should be open to all. Economic and social data collected by the government and not identifiable by individual or company ought also to be available to all who have an interest. But confidential or proprietary information that can be identified as relating to a particular individual or corporation must be carefully safeguarded.

The general principles may be clear, but their application to particular cases may present real difficulties. One case in point is the present proceeding before the Federal Power Commission looking toward closing to the public the hitherto available detailed record of fuel purchases by utilities. In this, the utilities, joined by the FTC and the antitrust division of Justice, seek to ban the publication of this information from a fear that it may support collusion or price-fixing about fuel suppliers; other interests believe, on the contrary, that it is essential this information be available to monitor prices, to justify utilities' cost figures for rate-making, and to oversee energy problems. If the Commission decides to withhold that data, one recently started newsletter, *Fuel Price Analysis,* will have to abandon publication. The demise of one newsletter may be relatively unimportant, but the principle *is* important—and too often industry does not get access to information it needs and deserves.

Generally in discussion of the government's policies toward its own information stores, business firms or associations express an interest only when they are directly affected by some particular action, and they are likely to confine their attention to that particular case. What we need, what the government needs, is input from the business community as to the guidelines that should control the government's policies and decisions throughout the whole areas of freedom of information and privacy.

When we are dealing with such enormous masses of data as those in the government's keeping, it is not a matter of access alone.

We of the business community need a watch service that can scan this endless flow of information, select the items of real interest, look behind them for their full meaning, analyze and interpret them, correlate them with other data from both public and private sources, bring them to the attention of those tens and hundreds of thousands of firms and executives in the business community.

This is the job the private-sector information companies, like our own and dozens of our competitors, undertake to perform. We do it in numbers of ways. One is by thorough, investigative, interpretive journalism in publications like *The Wall Street Journal* and *Business Week,* and in more specialized magazines such as *Chemical Week* or *Coal Age.*

Another way is by newsletters, giving very fast, "insider" news on specific areas of special interest, or even faster daily newswires.

Still another is by preparing bibliographies, indexes, abstracting services, and other guides to government material, arranged to serve the interests of the user.

The third way is by reformatting government materials so that, for example, it may be available in a more compact and less expensive microfilm or microfiche form.

A fourth is obtaining, or creating, machine-readable tapes of government data and offering on-line access to them through privately prepared programming and often in association with other data bases, so that the basic data can be organized, analyzed, and retrieved in ways that give them an added value to the user.

In all these ways private-sector information companies provide invaluable services to the business community. They are alert to every specialized need of that community. They act not for the government, disseminating what the government wants disseminated with the interpretations the government prefers. They act for that broader community, businessman and ordinary citizen alike, who depend on access to this sort of information to arrange our lives and carry on our business. The private-sector information business becomes the eyes and ears of the private sector.

Yet this private-sector information industry exists, in a sense, on government sufferance. The government may block its efforts by withholding information.

Even more frequent is the case when a government agency decides to go in the other direction, disseminating data to the public in ways directly competitive with services in which there has already been a substantial private investment.

For example, a private company, Congressional Information Service, offers all customers microfiche of Congressional hearings, reports, and other hard-to-get documents—a valuable and, because it's valuable, a profitable service. Now the Government Printing Office is planning a duplicate expense by offering similar microfiche to the six hundred key "depository" libraries for public documents, leaving the rest of the market unsupplied—yet taking, with tax-subsidized prices, so much of Congressional Information Service's core market as to make questionable its ability to offer the service to the remaining libraries, including corporate libraries.

Or consider the National Library of Medicine. Pharmaceutical companies and other private sector businesses got access to this enormous data base through a private company, Systems Development Corporation, which had obtained a license to disseminate the data. The NLM subsequently decided to serve the pharmaceutical companies directly, and at tax-subsidized prices well below what SDC had to charge, with an instant loss to SDC of this business and of its investment in the development of it. Nor was the Library of Medicine willing to sell or lease the tapes to SDC at rates that would make it possible for them to compete. Such an elimination of a private company from a total market through government competition in one sector of it may entirely deprive the rest of the market since neither the government nor the private competition may serve it.

In giving these random examples, I am not inviting sympathy for private-sector information companies, at least for the larger ones like ourselves. There is no law saying we have to enter or continue an unprofitable business, and of course we will not.

My concern here is a much more fundamental one. I believe very deeply that the control and management of information will become the major component of power in American society. Effective access to an efficient information system will be indispensable to the success of any business enterprise and indeed to any of the educational, governmental, or other enterprises of our society. The federal government already bestrides the world of information like a colossus. It collects and assembles the enormous bodies of economic data on which our business decisions depend. It records and controls the knowledge of the innumerable thousands of legislative, judicial, regulatory, and executive decisions that govern our lives. It supports much of the research out of which our technology grows and controls the mode of its dissemination. Out of all these stores of data, it decides what to release and what not and in what way.

Moreover, the government lays down the laws, determines the regulations, decides the policies under which all private-sector businesses operate. It is both ruler and competitor. It is capable of drawing to itself the enormous power that derives from the control of information.

I do not mean to suggest that this potential authority is exercised with any evil intent. On the contrary, I think most of those who are responsible for public policy want a governmental information policy that genuinely serves the public interest and is open to the operations of a healthy private-sector information economy.

The difficulties of the past and the risks of the future have been more likely to rise from inadvertence or unawareness than from hostile intent. Decisions may be made in one area of information policy without realization of their consequences in another area. Decisions may be allowed to slide because the appropriate persons are not yet aware that a problem exists. Certainly decisions are made without any adequate input from the business community at large because that community has not organized itself to offer any major input.

The next two or three years will be filled with decisions that will go far to shape our whole information structure for many, many years to come. I've already touched on the decisions facing us in the postal and telephone fields as well as government's role in the information field. There are others. A general revision of the Federal Communications

Act is being proposed. International negotiations to allocate the broadcast spectrum are just ahead. The security and freedom of transnational communication is an increasingly critical problem which we are only now beginning to face up to. These are only a few samples of the information policies which must soon be addressed.

It is terribly important that they be made in awareness of the totality of business interests as well as the interests of the other major sectors of American society. It is terribly important, too, that those decisions preserve a vigorous and far-reaching function for private-sector information operations that can provide a counterbalance to government power.

In reaching these decisions, it *is* essential that there be leaders in the government who are aware of this whole range of problems and of their interrelation, are dedicated to maintaining a free flow of information, and to strengthening a vital private-sector information industry.

Through recent discussions with key members of the executive branch, my colleagues and I are optimistic that there is such awareness, there is dedication to freedom, and appreciation for private-sector information services. Perhaps most important, they are interested in and open to your views. The executive branch, the Congress, and the FCC *are* hearing from companies with special interests in the information field. They are *not* getting input from businessmen generally to help them assess the impact of policy decisions on the business community as a whole.

The challenge is ours. I hope that in your respective corporations, within this Institute, and within other general business organizations there will be thoughtful consideration of these problems. And I hope you will bring your own views to appropriate decision-makers throughout government with energy and conviction.

A revolution need not be chaotic and destructive. It can represent a positive step forward. We are in the midst of an information revolution. Its outcome depends in good measure on how intelligently all of us approach it. That is the challenge facing us today.

Thank you.

THE FIRST AMENDMENT: FREEDOM AND RESPONSIBILITY[5]

CHARLES McC. MATHIAS, JR.[6]

Democratic society can function because of a "delicate balance of powers" between various divisions in government. In our own federal system a fragile equilibrium is maintained through a system of checks and balances in the three branches. As a further safeguard in a democratic society, philosophers and the framers of the Constitution envisioned an alert citizenry as the final arbitrator in cases where interests conflicted. To guarantee a continual free exchange of ideas and the monitoring of officials, the framers sought to promote free speech, free press, and the right of assembly in the First Amendment to the Constitution. Throughout our history we have celebrated and cherished the unique freedoms conferred upon us by the Constitution and the first ten amendments that comprise the Bill of Rights. Any action that is perceived as a threat to those freedoms—for example, the 1978 Supreme Court decision denying newspapers a special right to advance warning before court-approved searches—arouses strong protest.

On October 26, 1977, the Anti-Defamation League of B'nai B'rith presented its First Amendment Freedoms Award to John Cowles and his son John Cowles, Jr. The league established the award "to honor individuals and institutions, who by their words and deeds, give the First Amendment . . . their stalwart support." In bestowing the award on the Cowles family, the committee wished to recognize the contributions of the family that publishes the prestigious Des Moines *Register* and *Tribune* and the Minneapolis *Star* and *Tribune* and *Harper's Magazine* (the younger Cowles serves as a chairman of the board of Harper and Row). In a speech of introduction at the presentation, Senator Wendell R. Anderson (Democrat, Minnesota) referred to the two honorees as "gentlemen of strength and character who have always been a vital part, a constructive part of the community."

The main speaker, Senator Charles McC. Mathias, Jr. (Re-

[5] Delivered at the First Amendment Freedoms Awards dinner of the Anti-Defamation League of B'nai B'rith, Bloomington, Minnesota, October 26, 1977. Quoted by permission.

[6] For biographical note, see Appendix.

publican, Maryland) then addressed 575 civic and business leaders and media representatives from the Twin Cities area, assembled at the Radisson South Hotel in Bloomington, Minnesota. He reminded his listeners that the duty of the Fourth Estate is to keep the public informed, but he warned that the only check on the journalist was "the exercise of self-restraint." He cited the Cowles family and their editorial policies as exemplary in the exercise of this type of self-restraint. Perhaps in suggesting the relationship of freedom to responsibility, he adroitly called attention to what Wes Gallagher of the Associated Press told his colleagues at a meeting on May 3, 1976:

> The First Amendment is not a hunting license as some today seem to think. It is a privilege and a right we exercise on behalf of the public. Nor does it override all other constitutional protections. No right or privilege is absolute in a democracy. Each is dependent on the other. Absolute rights are claimed by kings and dictators. We are neither.

Not highly original in presenting new insights on freedom, the Mathias speech served rather to reaffirm faith in our system of government. To provide emotional appeal and to strengthen his arguments, Mathias included quotations from James Madison, Thomas Jefferson, Chief Justice Warren Burger, and Justice William J. Brennan, Jr. The simplicity of the speech enhanced its meaning and significance.

The two men we honor here—John Cowles and John Cowles, Jr.—interpret the First Amendment to the Constitution exactly as I think the framers of the Constitution intended. They recognize and accept the responsibility inherent in the broad grant of freedom the First Amendment gives the press.

John Cowles has said that "a good newspaper should be a university on your doorstep." He and his son have acted on that belief. They have built and run a communications network that actually tries to inform, not just to amuse, the public. For this, they richly deserve the Anti-Defamation League's "First Amendment Freedoms Award." As James Madison observed:

A popular Government, without popular information, or the means of acquiring it, is but a prologue to a farce or a tragedy or perhaps both. Knowledge will forever govern ignorance: and a people who mean to be their own governors must arm themselves with the power which knowledge gives.

This week the question of the responsibility of the press in a free society is very much in the news. On Sunday we learned for the first time the details of an effort by former CIA Director William E. Colby to suppress the Glomar Explorer story on the grounds of national security. So tonight it seems particularly appropriate to examine with you the very fragile relationship between press freedom and press responsibility which is central to our democracy and which the Cowles family has understood so well.

The preeminent place given to freedom of the press in the Bill of Rights—its placement, along with freedom of speech, in the first of the amendments to the Constitution —reflects its central role in the functioning of our republic. The founders of our republic considered the free expression of informed citizens to be the foundation of representative government. They far preferred the risk that a free press might abuse its freedom to the risks implicit in regulating the press.

The language of the First Amendment is simple and clear: "Congress shall make no law . . . abridging the freedom of speech, or of the press . . ."

The men who wrote the Constitution were not blind to the possibility that the press might abuse or misuse its power. Indeed, George Washington was one of the first public figures to feel the sting of a vicious, irresponsible press. But, even in the face of attack, Washington stuck to his conviction that no matter how the press might abuse its privileges, he considered it vital for the survival of democracy that press freedom not be curbed.

Here, in a letter to a friend Thomas Jefferson explains the view of the enlightened American leadership:

No experiment can be more interesting than that we are now trying, which we trust will end by establishing the fact that man may be governed by reason and truth.

Our first object should be therefore to leave open to him all avenues of truth. The most effectual hitherto found is the freedom of the press. It is therefore the first shut up by those who fear the investigation of their actions.

The firmness with which the people have withstood the late abuses of the press, the discernment they have manifested between truth and falsehood shew that they may safely be trusted to hear everything true and false and to form a correct judgment between them.

I don't think there's a better statement anywhere of our founders' conviction that the essential safeguard to free government was an alert public informed by a free press. A sublime confidence in the good sense of the citizenry is what brought about our experiment in democracy.

The notion that the press has a role to play in the process of government was not unique to America. When Louis XVI was forced to call into session the Estates General in France after more than one hundred years of autocratic rule, he summoned the three estates—the nobles, the clergy and the commoners. But there was another group in France then that, since the invention of the printing press, had become powerful enough to be considered a Fourth Estate. That group was the press.

Although the Fourth Estate never quite made it into the Estates General or its successor the National Assembly, it did become part of our language. The Western world acknowledges, by its use of the quaint expression "the Fourth Estate," that the press plays a significant role in government.

If we accept the proposition that the Fourth Estate is a part of practical government, then we must look for the place in which it fits in our geometric constitutional pattern. Our constitutional system of checks and balances is more than a simple separation of powers among the three branches. There is a delicate balance of powers, in which the executive is checked by the legislative, the legislative by the judicial, the judicial by the executive, and so on. It is a system in which the exercise of fragmented power is often an exercise in frustration. But, we must remember that it was deliberately designed that way.

The authors of the Constitution were extremely sensitive to human frailties. Even Jefferson, despite his abundant confidence in the people as a whole, was wary of power and its ability to corrupt. "In questions of power," he wrote, "let no more be heard of confidence in man, but bind him down by the chains of the Constitution."

The men who devised our Constitution were not content with a simple separation of powers among the three branches of the new government. They actually gave each branch a hand in the other's business. Although some specific powers were reserved peculiarly or preeminently to each branch, there was a great deal of overlapping and intermingling of jurisdictions within the three formal and established branches of government.

The history of our government, in fact, can be seen with some justice as a series of boundary disputes, of advances and retreats, between the various branches. Let us look at the way it has worked.

For example, the Constitution gives the President "power, by and with the Advice and Consent of the Senate, to make treaties . . ." George Washington, at first, was very direct in seeking the "Advice and Consent of the Senate." Thanks to the journal kept by Pennsylvania Senator William Maclay, we know that President Washington astounded the Senate on a humid Saturday in late August 1789 when he arrived at the Senate chambers, "was introduced, and took our Vice President's chair . . . rose and told us bluntly that he had called on us for our Advice and Consent to some propositions respecting the treaty to be held with the Southern Indians."

The Senate thought Washington was trying to railroad the treaty through and gave him a cool reception. The President, miffed that his overture had been rebuffed, left in what Maclay describes as a "violent fret" and never again appeared in person to ask the Senate for "Advice and Consent."

Since then, as far as I know, no other President has appeared in person looking for "Advice and Consent" of the Senate either. President Carter, in fact, was signing the Panama Canal Treaty at just about the same time as the Senate was first considering its text. But the point is that, no matter how the relationship between the President and the Senate changes, the Constitution assigns each a specific role in the treaty process and one acts as a check upon the other.

But where in this rather precise geometric construction of checks and balances is the Fourth Estate? The check which applies to that branch of governance we call the Fourth Estate is the First Amendment, which is a check on government unilaterally. The First Amendment prohibits interference with press activity just as much as the doctrine of separation of powers prevents the legislative, executive, and judicial branches of government from invading each other's jurisdictions.

But what of the other side of the equation? The First Amendment is only a one-sided check and does not provide balance. The other side doesn't exist. And, because there is no balancing factor as in the case of the other three Branches, we end up with a paradox. We restrain government in its relations with the press, but we don't restrain the press in its relations with government.

There's good reason for this. The restraints which we impose on the executive, legislative, and judicial branches of government cannot be imposed upon the press without endangering the democratic process itself. Freedom of the press is an area too sensitive and too delicate to sustain external regulation. And, as Chief Justice Burger has noted:

A responsible press is an undoubtedly desirable goal, but press responsibility is not mandated by the Constitution and like many other virtues cannot be legislated.

It seems to me that the only restraint on the press that is permissible in a democracy is the restraint the press imposes on itself. The press, in a very real sense, is a part of the government. By providing much of the information on which the electorate makes its judgments, the press plays an essential role in determining how, and how well, we govern ourselves. If we are to govern ourselves intelligently, then the media must be free to gather information and to disseminate it without hindrance. But, it is not enough that the media be free to do their job, they must also be willing to do it responsibly.

We cannot force the media to exercise self-restraint. But we can commend outstanding examples of media responsibility as you are doing here tonight. And organizations such as the Anti-Defamation League can encourage responsible journalism.

In April 1735, John Peter Zenger established for the first time in an American court the right of the press to criticize the government. Since then that right has been confirmed and reconfirmed in the courts. We have, in the words of Justice Brennan:

> . . . a profound national commitment to the principle that debate on public issues should be uninhibited, robust and wide-open, and that it may well include vehement, caustic, and sometimes unpleasantly sharp attacks on government and public officials . . .
>
> (*New York Times Co. v. Sullivan*)

I am sure all here would agree with me that the press has more than earned its First Amendment protection these past four years. The word "Watergate" alone conjures up memories of press heroics that will not soon be forgotten. And the media have bolstered our liberties in many other areas as well.

But what I think we do tend to forget in the glow of so many recent Fourth Estate victories is that there is always someone lying in wait for a chance to clip the wings of the press.

It is worth remembering that only nine years after the Bill of Rights had been adopted, Congress passed the infamous Alien and Sedition Act of 1798. Or to bring the story closer to this time and this place, let me read you what Vice President Spiro Agnew said of the press right here in Minneapolis less than five years ago:

> . . . some prestigious media spokesmen can be read and heard almost daily expressing fear for the future of the First Amendment. They assert that the American people are being kept in the dark by a deceptive government. A national network newsman has referred to an Administration "conspiracy" against the people's right to know. It is hard to find any factual basis for this hysteria. Almost nothing goes on in government that is not examined, re-examined, plumbed, analyzed, guessed about, criticized and caricatured by the media.
> . . . The fact is that the Nixon Administration is no more desirous of nor more capable of curtailing freedom of the press in America than any of its predecessors. . . .
>
> (Before Minnesota Newspaper Association, Minneapolis, February 23, 1973)

The Administration conspiracy against the people's right to know which Agnew dismisses here as press hysteria, was, of course, real. Even with all the forces of the Nixon Administration arrayed against them, however, the "nattering nabobs of negativism," to borrow Agnew's own idiom, won the day.

But next time we may not be so lucky. If our luck is to hold, it is important that the media remain alert to their unwritten responsibilities under the First Amendment. And it is important that we, as a people, remain sensitive to efforts to curtail the freedom of the press.

After all, as David Brinkley once said:

There are numerous countries in the world where the politicians have seized absolute power and muzzled the press. But there is no country in the world where the press has seized absolute power and muzzled the politicians.

PARTING THOUGHTS[7]

ERIC SEVAREID[8]

On November 30, 1977, Walter Cronkite, anchorman for the CBS Evening News, announced, "After a forty-six-year career—thirty-eight of them with CBS News and the last fourteen as a regular contributor to this broadcast—Eric Sevareid retires tonight. Here are his parting thoughts." The moment was an emotional one for Sevareid and his many listeners.

Tom Shales of the Washington *Post* (November 30, 1977) described Sevareid as "a knight of an old order" and suggested that his departure signaled "the demise of the broadcast commentator and perhaps of the gentleman journalist as well." The passing fraternity that Sevareid represented included, from radio and television, H. V. Kaltenborn, Elmer Davis, and Edward R. Murrow (who trained Sevareid), and from the print media, Walter Lippmann and James Reston. Men of integrity and dignity, these journalists witnessed the great events of World War II and the dramatic events of the following years. They attracted listeners and readers because they gave meaning and dimension to passing events.

Generally, persons who listened to Sevareid concentrated on what he had to say rather than upon his personality or delivery. A reporter observed that "virtually all of TV's newspeople" are "essentially more important as personalities than they are as professional news gatherers. They are news" (Fred Feretti, New York *Times,* February 5, 1978). But Sevareid was not showy, and no one could accuse him of being "news."

Not a flamboyant media personality, Sevareid was, instead, sober, well-informed, and meditative. Charles Kuralt said, "Eric went from facts to intelligence to wisdom." In two to three minutes within a half-hour broadcast, he attempted to make sense of a new development, a political happening, or a world calamity in the manner of a professor or thoughtful bystander. Sevareid always chose "his own subjects" without any interference from his colleagues. After thinking about his topic most of the day, he

[7] Delivered from CBS studios, Washington, D.C. Copyright, CBS Inc., 1977. All rights reserved. Originally broadcast November 30, 1977, over CBS Television Network as part of the CBS Evening News. Quoted by permission.

[8] For biographical note, see Appendix.

typed it out for his evening appearance, "seldom revising, changing not a word." A secretary then transferred the script to a teleprompter (Robert Gregory, "Signing Off" from *Passage,* quoted in the *Congressional Record,* October 28, 1977, p S18111). In speaking of the pitfalls in this procedure, Sevareid revealed: "As a result, you're bound to sound terribly positive and almost smug. That is part of the price of compression; it gives you no chance to loosen up a bit. And of course I look like the great stone face anyway" (quoted by Tom Shales).

Ending his final broadcast as he always had, the "somber, stony-faced" commentator said: "This was Eric Sevareid in Washington. Thank you and good-bye."

By my time of life one has accumulated more allegiances and moral debts than the mind can remember or the heart contain. So I cannot enumerate my betters, my mentors and sustainers during so many years of trying to use, with sense, this communications instrument, as unperfected as the persons who use it. But they know that I know who they are. Many are gone, including the man who invented me, Ed Murrow; some died in the wars we were reporting. I've gone the normal span of a man's working life, rather abnormal in this calling, and it's a happy surprise.

We were like a young band of brothers in those early radio days with Murrow. If my affections are not easily given, neither are they easily withdrawn. I have remained through it all with CBS News, and if it is regarded as old fashioned to feel loyalty to an organization, so be it. Mine has been here an unelected, unlicensed, uncodified office and function. The rules are self-imposed. These were a few: Not to underestimate the intelligence of the audience and not to overestimate its information; to elucidate when one can, more than to advocate; to remember always that the public is only people and people only persons, no two alike; to retain the courage of one's doubts, as well as one's convictions, in this world of dangerously passionate certainties; to comfort oneself in times of error with the knowledge that the saving grace of the press, print or broadcast is its self-correcting nature; and to remember that ignorant and biased reporting has its counterpart in ignorant and biased reading and listening. We do not speak into an intellectual or emotional void.

One's influence cannot be measured. History provides for the journalist no markers or milestones, but he's allowed to take his memories. And one can understand, as he looks back, the purpose of the effort and why it must be done. A friend and teacher, the late Walter Lippmann, described the role of the professional reporter and observer of the news in this manner: "We make it our business," he said, "to find out what is going on, under the surface and beyond the horizon; to infer, to deduce, to imagine and to guess what is going on inside—and what this meant yesterday and what it could mean tomorrow. In this way we do what every sovereign citizen is supposed to do but has not the time or the interest to do it for himself. This is our job. It is no mean calling and we have the right to be proud of it and to be glad that it is our work."

In the end, of course, it is not one's employers or colleagues that sustain one quite so much as the listening public, when it be so minded. And I have found that it applies only one consistent test: not agreement with one on substance, but the perception of honesty and fair intent. There is in the American people a tough, undiminished instinct for what is fair. Rightly or wrongly, I have the feeling that I have passed that test. I shall wear this like a medal. Millions have listened, intently and indifferently, in agreement and in powerful disagreement. Tens of thousands have written their thoughts to me. I will feel always that I stand in their midst.

This was Eric Sevareid in Washington. Thank you and good-bye.

WHITHER THE HUMANITIES

GENERAL EDUCATION: THE ROLE OF THE HUMANITIES [1]

JOSEPH D. DUFFEY [2]

On October 24 and 25, 1977, the University of Rhode Island held a conference on general education. The planners set forth the purpose of the meeting as follows:

> The goal of the conference is to challenge our thinking about the purpose of general education at URI. We need to redefine the nature of general education, and how it relates to liberal education and professional education and to decide what the role of general education should be within the total university curriculum. Most importantly, we need to know how, indeed if, general education prepares students for productive and meaningful lives.

Lately such concerns have been discussed frequently on college campuses. General education and the humanities have been put on the defensive—enrollments in these subject areas have been decreasing and funding is increasingly tied to enrollment. Those subjects that attract students receive the most support, and those that do not are dropped from the college curriculum. A fundamental question is, "Should career education be substituted for general education?"

There is no one more qualified to give advice on such matters than Joseph D. Duffey, newly appointed chairman of the National Endowment for the Humanities. His agency provides funding for many cultural activities throughout the country. On October 24, 1977, at 8 P.M. at Chafee Center on the campus at the University of Rhode Island he spoke to an audience of faculty members, students, and interested citizens.

This occasion provided him with the opportunity to make one of his first statements concerning the humanities since his

[1] Delivered at the Finkelstern Lecture at the Conference on General Education, Chafee Center, University of Rhode Island, 8 P.M., October 24, 1977. Quoted by permission.

[2] For biographical note, see Appendix.

appointment. The address was noteworthy and closely attended. In the first half of his speech, Duffey discussed the benefits that the humanities can contribute to students:

> To the preparation of students for their lives as productive members of this society, the humanities add not merely habits of mental acuity but priceless attributes of self-awareness and social responsibility. They make of the educational process an initiation into the exercise of moral character in addition to the acquisition of knowledge and skills.

To the question, "How do we distinguish 'wisdom and judgment' from 'prejudice, irrational instinct and popular fancy?' " Duffey replied that "the humanistic insight can become . . . a path of intellectual liberation from the social world which surrounds us and tries to lock us into particular ways of thinking."

In the second half of the speech, he considered the role of humanities in society at large and he advanced an argument for the application of the humanities to aspects of life outside the university. He also argued that "the gifts . . . humanities can offer us" are "a clearer awareness of alternatives, a healthy respect at once for human understanding and for uncertainty, a chance to disengage from coercive and parochial communities, and an invitation to join a broader and more-inclusive one built around concerns which are crucial to contemporary society." Later on, Duffey made the suggestion that "college teachers . . . consider the interweavings of the powerful strands of their thought with the fabric of ordinary life as it is lived in America today." At least some members of his audience at the University of Rhode Island took exception to this view concerning the popularization of the humanities. (For a position similar to that of Duffey, the reader should consult the speech by Robert Coles, below.)

Joseph D. Duffey read his speech from manuscript. He was "low key and contemplative" in his delivery, resembling more the philosopher than a politician. He found his listeners more "receptive" to his formal remarks than to his responses during the question and answer period. One observer reported, "Some felt it [the speech] was a bit cliché, perhaps more political and philosophical versus substantive and pragmatic" (letter from Richard A. Katula of the University of Rhode Island, March 23, 1978).

When Timothy Dwight, president of Yale, passed through this area in 1800, he noted that South Kingston was a prosperous farming area—and I see it still is.

But President Dwight also remarked that the inhabitants were "generally uncouth, their manners tending to intemperance, their houses unkempt." "Schools in this state," he wrote, "can hardly be said to exist."

I'm glad to be able today to retract completely such scurrilous impressions! I am also delighted to be here with you.

I am honored by the invitation to participate in your effort to redefine the role of general education at the University of Rhode Island.

We are committed to a similar task at the National Endowment for the Humanities trying to, as your documents here put it, make "the communication of a sense of civilization" a priority among Americans.

You are revising a curriculum, and I am overseeing a federal agency; many of the problems you have addressed here today, we have in common.

We share such questions as:

"How shall we define general education?"

"What are the humanities?"

"Shall we pursue excellence as a single priority or shall we be concerned as well with the question of access: of the public's right to learn and to know?"

These inquiries are the very essence of the humanistic tradition. They are at the heart of the questions which have shaped our culture for thousands of years.

As a way of looking at the nature of these questions, we can compare them with the technical problems we face at the same time.

When we address the issues of curriculum design in the technical sense, we are first inclined to look for parallel cases elsewhere. We ask friends from graduate school days, read professional journals, confer (endlessly)—and more and more these days, we appeal to electronic data retrieval systems to find models for our case.

With technical problems our effort is to locate gaps in our knowledge:

How to schedule courses and requirements. How to staff them.

As little time as possible is spent at this point in asking whether the whole enterprise is worth something, and to whom.

Our fundamental concern is getting the right information, getting the data, gathering the fruits of a system of experts and consultants.

As you have no doubt become aware, however, the technical problems and implementation do not exhaust the subject of curriculum revision.

No matter how much information we have, or how much we refine it, there always remain the nagging conflicts, the gaps which no technical data can fill: between process and product, between excellence and equality.

These are the questions that do not get easier the more we know about them, which are problems not capable of total resolution.

The temptation in a society such as ours which prizes efficiency is to bracket these more profound questions of meaning and purpose and set them aside as we go about our business.

No data bank is available to provide answers to these questions.

The requisite tools seem to be those qualities of mind we call wisdom, judgment, experience and intuition.

But this is a great irony. If we had wisdom and judgment enough to use in solving our problems, then presumably we would not have such problems.

How do we get judgment—and how do we distinguish it from prejudice, irrational instinct, and popular fancy?

This is, I believe, where we touch the role of the humanities. It is not an easy process, to be sure, and one which can never be completed. But there is no sounder way to confront the crucial moral and philosophical issues we face than to see these questions in the light of the historical culture we share as a people.

How are we to explore these problems in a humanistic way?

Take the issue of excellence vs. equality. In some sense, this is only a variant of the age-old problem of the place of justice in the political community. Might not therefore Thucydides and Aristotle, Machiavelli and Adam Smith, John Rawls and Robert Nozick be as helpful as commentators on our situation as contemporary university administrators?

If we are concerned with understanding how communities of scholars respond to situations of crisis, would not our insight be aided by looking at the experience of European universities during the Reformation or African Universities during the 1960s?

We do not, I think, denigrate the humanities, when we see them in such intimacy with the problems we meet in our everyday lives.

The richness of our culture is too important to be merely an ornament of our lives, to be worn as a badge of social or moral superiority. Nor is the tradition we uphold merely a refuge from the world, a private stock of inspiration or solace to help us withstand the pressures of social life.

The humanities can and ought to claim a more active, public role as a living, breathing confrontation with the ways we make sense of human life.

The benefits of humanistic learning cannot of course be measured in simple utilitarian or instrumental terms. Understanding our problems better is not necessarily the fastest or most economical way of solving them.

But the benefits are nonetheless substantial, and I want to take some time and some care to outline my view of them for you.

What are the benefits of the humanistic perspective? Let

me suggest five distinct but related contributions to learning.

For one thing, the perspective of the humanities may refine and sharpen our questions by setting them in the context of the past.

When we go to the great thinkers, the lessons they teach are not simple or one-sided or direct. In fact, they often pose more questions than answers.

For every Jansenist view of human finitude, there is a Jesuit call for energy and self-reliance.

For every Hegelian spiritualization of truth and history, there is a corresponding Nietzschean emphasis upon human willfulness.

But out of facing complexity may come a habit of mind which accepts contradiction and learns to anticipate objections. We learn to seek illumination, rather than to build forts and trenches of thought. We learn to be humbled but not unnerved by ambiguity and uncertainty.

A slightly different way of saying the same thing is that the humanistic tradition trains us to recognize that something of value is always lost in the advent of anything new and this is the second contribution of humanistic learning.

It is hard to imagine that our urban planning fiascos of post-war years would have gone forward if there had been some sense that the communities being "renewed" needed to be protected against loss as much as aided from the outside.

Their lack of proper housing or schools or jobs—and not in terms of what they still possessed—networks of family and community relationships, pride and place and a healthy skepticism toward the benevolence of outsiders. Today we are at work trying to correct the errors of earlier misunderstandings.

The experience of Vietnam was a further and more tragic example of the same fundamental errors in judgment and wisdom.

So infatuated had we become with our own intentions for the Vietnamese and for their country that when we noted the discrepancies between their reality and our designs, we saw them only as justifications for a greater commitment to fulfill those designs.

Frances Fitzgerald demonstrates in her superb book, *Fire in the Lake,* how American planners almost invariably misunderstood the complex cultural assumptions of rural Vietnamese farmers. Fitzgerald's analysis is based upon careful research into the social and cultural background of Indochina. But I suspect that a serious and honest awareness of the distinctiveness of any alien culture might have produced more caution among our policy-makers.

That these men were so often the products of our most elite liberal arts colleges and universities makes even more urgent the case for understanding the relevance of the humanities as a way of instilling us with an awareness of what may sometimes be lost in our efforts to effect change.

Professor Morton Bloomfield of Harvard has expressed the insight I want to convey here. He wrote recently (*Daedalus,* Fall, 1974):

> Action becomes blind and meaningless unless it is backed by perspective and knowledge. Although perspective and knowledge can and often do lead to inaction, they can also lead to action. What does being contemporary mean? It means knowing what alternatives are open to one and what can be done without destroying what is worthwhile. This knowledge comes only from reflection and from a knowledge of tradition . . .

My third observation is this: In all the great strands of our humanistic inheritance there is an admonition to caution and to intellectual humility.

Where the technical world is always seeking to reduce, to set limits, and even to eliminate uncertainty, the humanist cherishes that element of mystery as much as he or she does the positive knowledge acquired in its face.

In all the great literatures of the past, a fundamental attitude of mind is upheld: being fully alert to oneself, attentive to all the nerve endings of our being, and yet at the same time fully receptive to the wisdom of the world, humbly awaiting and welcoming its meanings for us.

This is the way of Baconian Empiricism, the way of what Buddhists call "Vijn-Ana," the quality which Evangelical Christians know as "conviction." Keats spoke of this when he attributed to Shakespeare something called "negative capability." "Man is capable," he wrote, "of being in uncertainties, mysteries, (and) doubts, without any irritable reaching after fact and reason."

Despite all the differences between these terms, they share a respect for the fearless human apprehension of uncertainties, and ironic willingness to be totally present without imposing oneself on the world blindly.

The key word in the humanistic disciplines is attention, and it is worth remembering its root—an old French verb meaning *to stretch to* something. Stretching, not shrinking—in the face of uncertainty is what all of us need to do.

My fourth observation about the contribution of the humanities would be that—one of the ways we experience this uncertainty is to look at the same phenomenon from several different vantage points.

The demographer, for example, might look at the state of Rhode Island as a population with certain characteristics of settlement, size, fertility, employment and literacy. (Even as Timothy Dwight did!)

How different will be the view in the eyes of the geologist, the geographer, the economist, the ecologist, the student of literature, the anthropologist, the political scientist, the historian.

I do not want to argue that one discipline is more correct than another. The humanistic tradition stands apart, in a sense, from all of these perspectives. I want to point out instead how the juxtaposition of all these fields, addressed to the same subject is a constant process of focusing and refocusing our perception of reality.

We might understand the humanities as the overlap of these distinct disciplines, or what has often been called interdisciplinary inquiry. But I would rather define the humanistic insight as the sense of widening and narrowing our vision—as the serious inquiry which proceeds when we stand outside each of the disciplines and witness the limits of each.

Each of these perspectives tells us something about Rhode Island, but each has a specific history and depends on a social world for its support. By standing apart from each of them, the humanities allows us to assume what some sociologists call a "theoretic stance" toward all of them.

To put it simply, each of these perspectives or disciplines is a human invention. Each of these views is the construction of a particular society.

Even though we experience Rhode Island and the rest of the world through particular glasses, it is at least theoretically possible for us to doff these spectacles and see the lenses themselves for what they are, devices for investigating our world and our place within it.

The idea that our knowledge is part of a social construction, the underlying premise of what has been called the sociology of knowledge, has been developing rapidly since the eighteenth century Italian historian Giovanni Battista Vico began to assess historical progression as a human artifact.

This insight is central to the work of Marx and Michelet, Durkheim, Freud and Weber, indeed to a major tradition of the social sciences over the past two centuries.

There are those who see the sociology of knowledge as hostile to the way we have interpreted the humanistic tradition as a continuing, even timeless, aspect of thought.

But recognizing that the things we know are always the product of a particular society does not reduce the value of knowing them, any more than the eternal conflicts between the Platonist and the Aristotelian make it unnecessary to pay attention to either.

By understanding the contingency of our particular ways of thinking as late twentieth century Americans, we gain some distance from ourselves, some perspective on who we are and how much value we can attach to our limited points of view.

The humanistic insight can become, then, a path of intellectual liberation from the social world which surrounds us and tries to lock us into particular ways of thinking which mesh with its own limited definition of "reality."

Within the disciplines and professions and cultural perspectives of our lives, we are attached to specific social forms, with hierarchies and methods of dissemination and evaluation. When we adopt the perspective of the humanities, we are—at least for the moment of epiphany—released from the grip of these systems of thought. Not released into a chaotic and undisciplined mental confusion but into a humble clarity about the boundedness of what we happen to know.

Finally, and in a more positive view, the perspective of the humanities offers us another community to supplant the one we escape in departing from the narrower perspectives of our individual disciplines.

I do not mean by this community the world of upper-class social privilege with which the pursuit of the higher culture was so long associated in American life. One of the most profound and beneficial effects of the "counter-culture" of the 1960s was the assault upon this association, upon the role of elite social groups as quasi-official guardians of the arts and humanities.

The community I have in mind is made up of those who are committed to over-stepping the limits of their own pressing technical concerns, who seek to make connections between problems in their fields of concern and those of people in different areas of endeavor, in different social classes, with different enthusiasms.

In a time of intense specialization, the tradition of the humanities offers perhaps the only field of concern where men and women of differing professions and social location can participate in a broader community of concern.

Many of the most critical issues we face today cannot be adequately addressed by technical learning alone. Or alone by communities of highly skilled professionals.

The issue of how we define educational excellence or what goals we set for our educational system are broad social questions which must be resolved by a community larger than that of the professional associations. And the same is true of national health insurance and the use of energy resources.

These questions are central to all our lives, and central to the critical traditions of this culture. Do not all of us, either as professionals or citizens, have a contribution to make to such discussions?

I do not hesitate to suggest to you that issues of everyday life in this society are rooted in our humanistic culture. At its heart, therefore, every activity in contemporary America—every moment of making and unmaking, of work and leisure, of learning and the passing on of learning—is also potentially an inquiry, an open-ended dialogue with the tradition we share.

Now, I don't pretend that every worker and farmer and administrator and housekeeper and salesperson and student does or could spend large portions of each day contemplating the fundamental questions being addressed in his or her work. But the challenge to do so, to read all of our distinct social conditions as cases of a larger inquiry into the human condition, is there. And all of us share the responsibility of making it possible for all our citizens to participate in that inquiry.

The easier path or course is to construe one's problems as belonging to a special province, capable of being understood only by other insiders or initiates, only by those with proper expertise or who share the same ethnic or religious background.

But perhaps the time has come to understand the commonality of our cultural inheritance as well as our pluralism. The struggle for dignity of a black family on welfare in an eastern city, a white lower-middle-class family hard-pressed to pay for college tuition, a midwestern farmer who has overinvested in capital equipment, is in many ways the same struggle, and the definitions of dignity offered by each have their roots in the same vision of human freedom and peace and excellence, in the same desire to inhabit what James Joyce once called "the fair courts of life."

That vision, and hence the community which shares it, are the products of our humanistic inheritance.

These, then, are the gifts which I believe the humanities can offer us—a clearer awareness of alternatives, a healthy respect at once for human understanding and for uncertainty, a chance to disengage from coercive and parochial communities, and an invitation to join a broader and more-inclusive one built around concerns which are crucial to contemporary society.

If these gifts are to be secured, the academic community has a major role to play.

As one of the most important agents of the preservation of our cultural heritage, the university has the responsibility of bringing to life in each generation the great minds of the past.

Through its more specialized studies, the terms of our dialogue with those minds is constantly reshaped. Those studies need the support of all Americans if we are to maintain access to the insight and learning of those who have gone before us.

There are other implications of this view of the humanities for our institutions of higher learning.

As our society becomes more technically sophisticated, and as the market for scholars and teachers continues to decline, it seems increasingly likely that almost all of our graduates will find their life work outside the world of school and colleges.

Perhaps paradoxically, then, universities more and more need to insist that undergraduate students encounter this critical tradition. With proportionately fewer graduates in liberal arts majors, and with a greater technical background required for employment, and with fewer opportunities for students to spend their mid-twenties bouncing around in search of experience, direction, and inspiration—the undergraduate years have become more important as the time to try out the connections between humanistic insight and workaday concerns.

I would guess, as some of you evidently have, that simply mandating several required courses in the development of Western philosophy or art or political history is not sufficient to make these connections.

Can we do more?

Can we ask college teachers to consider the interweavings of the most powerful strands of their thought with the fabric of ordinary life as it is lived in America today?

Can our college faculties, with all their trials about academic tenure and mandatory retirement and accountability, be relied upon to provide insight and sympathy for what lies ahead for students in the world beyond the college gates?

If, for example, the issue of loyalty will be encountered by our graduates most dramatically in their future jobs, in their ways of responding to the demands and rewards of large organizations, are our professional political theorists prepared to help them understand the relevance of Augustine or Thoreau or Kafka to the problems of corporate society?

If we are concerned with the shoddiness of our products and our programs, do we have the aestheticians and economists in our midst to tell us how and why our standards of workmanship are wanting?

If Americans are worried about the visual pollution of our environment, are there architectual historians, students of the ancient and medieval city, and cultural geographers to help inform our discourse about the contexts of our habitation?

If we are perplexed about the blurred distinctions between the sacred and the profane in contemporary film and the media, and confused about how to convey moral values to our children, are there anthropologists, students of religion and literature, or psychologists who can bring some reason to this dilemma?

Or is the professional humanist—a term used quite often in NEH literature—to become more professional than humanist? More concerned with the issues of his own discipline, to the exclusion of those we share as a culture?

If the academic community is to help preserve the spirit of the humanities as well as its matter, then it has to be asked fairly in our generation—as it was in that of Socrates and Rabelais and of Emerson's—whether our formal institutions of learning are capable of fulfilling these larger public responsibilities to our culture.

Let me be clear. I am not arguing that the university should become a "service station" for society, an advisory board for every practical problem facing Americans. Nor should every professor abandon his scholarship in favor of a magazine journalist's commentary on our social life.

Rather I want to urge academics to see their scholarship, teaching and community service as a part of this deeper, more common inquiry which we all possess.

Perhaps the best way of saying this is that, if the issues of contemporary life are rooted in the humanities, as I have claimed, then it is equally true that our knowledge is rooted in our social circumstances.

The treasure of our common learning is not, then, simply passed from the university, the library and the museum *to* the general public; it moves in both directions, the experience of the society informing our understanding as much as the other way around.

In no other way, I believe, can we defend our common

learning than by widening the opportunity to participate in it. Each person who reads Jane Austen, and who discovers and articulates something personally significant about her work, is also a contributing member of this culture. To be sure, the Jane Austen we understand is not the same one who wrote in the West Country of England a century-and-a-half ago—fortunately we have scholars of English literature to remind us of that constantly. But we are not unfaithful if we bring our fullest attentiveness (and our fullest sense of our own questions today) to her work.

Against the argument that such literature has no inherent social value and must be cherished as "art for art's sake," we have to protest that society has the obligation to seek wisdom wherever it can.

The great pleasure of the classics, after all, is the way they spur new insights, the way they respond to new concerns, in each generation.

We have, therefore, not only Shakespeare's *Hamlet* to enjoy, but Coleridge's "Hamlet" and Hazlitt's "Hamlet," and that of Ernest Jones and George Lyman Kittredge and J. Dover Wilson, and that of Oliver and Burton and Scofield.

And if a young reader were to look at Hamlet's confusion about playing the role of a loyal prince, a revenging son, a lover and a man of contemplation, and see in that confusion a mirror of his own modern perplexities about role, then would not the *Hamlet* tradition itself be nurtured by such use?

In the Act establishing the National Endowment for the Humanities a dozen years ago, Congress boldly proclaimed that "Democracy demands wisdom and vision in its citizens."

That sets rather high goals for the agency I now lead, for we are charged not only with supporting humanistic learning, but with encouraging Americans to use that learning in becoming wise and farsighted.

It is probably easier to achieve the former than the latter, easier to assist in the growth of our culture than to nurture its wisdom.

The Acts establishing the National Endowments, after all, were only a part of an extraordinary explosion of the cultural richness of American life in the last quarter-century.

The Economic vicissitudes plaguing academic institutions these days should not obscure the remarkable growth and development of American scholarship and the arts during this period.

Or the astonishing growth of museums and libraries, of publishing and the media, as ways of making this culture accessible to more of our citizens.

Or the splendid efforts to preserve America's past—in our historic buildings and districts, in the oral history of ethnic and folk societies, in our documentary and artifact collections.

Or, not least, in the amazing ability of institutions like this one to quadruple its student population in the last twenty years in order to help young Americans take their places as participants in this cultural explosion.

Has all of this growth made us wiser, more compassionate, more attentive as people?

This must be the meaning and purpose of our humanistic learning in the years ahead. The survival of our democratic community, especially in a technical age, is dependent upon the success of the humanities in nurturing our common culture.

To the preparation of students for their lives as productive members of this society, the humanities add not merely habits of mental acuity but priceless attributes of self-awareness and social responsibility. They make of the educational process an initiation into the exercise of moral character in addition to the acquisition of knowledge and skills.

Perhaps the most telling analogy for the transformation we seek comes from the experience of historic preservation. Twenty-five years ago and earlier, when we saved an historic structure, it was generally to be made into a museum, a shrine, the repository of an older and often an elite culture, which had to be rescued from the disruptive commercial and industrial growth around it.

Today we are preserving—in Rhode Island as much as anywhere—those industrial and commercial districts which were so recently viewed only as eyesores. And we preserve them not as sanctuaries from modern life but as places in which to live and work, to shop and converse and be creative. In the same way I hope that our whole humanistic tradition can come to *House* our most creative efforts to make this a beautiful and a just society.

A "LARGER VISION" OF THE HUMANITIES [3]

ROBERT COLES [4]

The swearing-in ceremony of Joseph D. Duffey as chairman of the National Endowment for the Humanities on October 18, 1977, was more than the usual pro-forma exercise conducted by lower-level dignitaries. On this day, before a large audience, the Carter Administration intended "a symbolic gesture meant in part to underscore the Administration's allegiance to cultural affairs." The appointment of Duffey—long involved in Democratic party activities—brought charges that President Carter had "politicized" the Humanities Endowment and its sister agency the Arts Endowment (Lon Tuck, Washington *Post,* October 19, 1977). To give status to the occasion, Vice President Walter F. Mondale administered the oath and made a brief speech in answer to critics of the appointment. He said pointedly: "Those who say that politics and culture do not mix have missed an important point about both disciplines. No serious sudent of these issues has ever suggested that aesthetic or academic questions should be decided by politicians or bureaucrats."

The swearing-in ceremony also took on additional symbolic significance. Instead of making an acceptance speech, Duffey invited four leaders in cultural affairs to speak briefly on the diverse conceptions of the "humanities." The distinguished panel included Isabel Charles, Dean of the College of Arts and Letters at the University of Notre Dame and a literary critic; Robert Coles, psychiatrist at Harvard University and a Pulitzer Prize author; G. Alexander Heard, Chancellor of Vanderbilt University; and M. Carl Holman, president of the National Urban League and a poet. Each of these presentations is worthy of consideration (see *Congressional Record,* January 7, 1978, p E7526-9), but only the Coles speech is reproduced in this volume.

Coles sets the humanities on a large screen, showing their importance in many facets of our society and encompassing a field far broader than book learning. He asks the National Endow-

[3] Delivered at the swearing-in ceremony of Joseph D. Duffey, as chairman of the National Endowment for the Humanities, in the auditorium of the Executive Office Building, White House, Washington, D.C., October 18, 1977. Title supplied by editor. Quoted by permission.

[4] For biographical note, see Appendix.

ment for the Humanities to "strive to do justice to the richness, the diversity of cultural life in a nation whose people are not . . . afraid to say what is on their minds, . . ." The humanities, says Coles, can be seen in the every day lives of all sorts of people, in the novels of William Faulkner, in jazz and gospel songs, and in impressionist art, as well as in "the sayings and memories and rituals of countless millions of working people" and in the traditional stories and songs of regional and ethnic groups. They come of the effort to make moral, philosophical, spiritual sense of this world.

Coles points out that "the humanities come into play" when the scientist or social scientist "starts wondering about . . . himself or herself—the person who has made a discovery, who lives . . . with and by some larger vision of things." He lets the extended testimony of an unnamed American worker communicate his meaning that anyone can qualify as a humanist in the struggle "for decency and integrity and generosity in the face of inevitable self-centeredness (the sin of pride)."

Robert Coles is a man of many sides. Pursuing his interest in social psychiatry, he has made field studies in the Deep South, New Mexico, and New England. He is a contributing editor to the *New Republic* and *American Poetry* and a member of the editorial board of the *American Scholar*. Scientist, author, and humanist, he demonstrates in his writing understanding and compassion for human aspirations, fantasies, suffering, and misfortune. He has earned the right to speak meaningfully of the spirit of the humanities.

The humanities were once regarded as "polite learning": the study of grammar, rhetoric, and especially, the classics. We could do worse than encourage such study among our young—so many of whom badly need to know how to write clearly, logically, coherently; and badly need to understand what Socrates kept reminding his students: that the truly wise person knows, among other things, how little he or she knows, how much remains to be learned. It is a sad day, our day, that brings a declining adequacy with the English language on the part of many school children, along with their constant exposure to the crudities of certain television programs, not to mention the idiotic and pretentious social science jargon that has worked its way into various "curricula."

Our lives in twentieth century America are dominated by the natural sciences; every time we turn a light switch, get into a car, receive penicillin, we silently acknowledge the influence of engineers, physicists, chemists on our everyday assumptions. The so-called social sciences, on occasion prematurely, have tried to follow suit—tell us that they, also, have begun learning how to master at least some realms of the universe: psychological and sociological riddles, as opposed to those posed by organic and inorganic matter, or the distant constellations of stars. Still, it has not been altogether a blessing for America's sectarian culture—this technological mastery enabled by the natural sciences, coupled with the increasing conviction of social scientists that our habits and thoughts will soon enough yield to one or another interpretive scheme. Kierkegaard's nineteenth century grievance—that the increased knowledge of his time enabled people to understand, or think they would soon understand, just about everything, except how to live a life—might well be our complaint as well. We have our hands on the energy of the atom; we have dozens of notions of why people do things as they do; but many of us have forgotten to ask what we really believe in, what we ought try to *be,* in contrast to *do.*

The natural sciences offer us much needed answers, solutions. The social sciences, now and then, offer us helpful explanations—along with, occasionally, a good deal of dreary, pompous, overwrought language. The humanities, in the hands of some, can also come down, finally, to precious, bloated and murky prose. But the humanities at their best give testimony to man's continuing effort to make moral, philosophical, spiritual sense of this world—to evoke its complexity, its many-sided nature; its ironies, inconsistencies, contradictions, and ambiguities. The humanities begin, for a scientist, when he or she starts asking what a particular fact or discovery will mean for those who want to comprehend the obligations, the responsibilities of citizenship—the possibilities and limitations a given society presents. The humanities come into play, for a social scientist, when he or she starts wondering what some observation or theoretical construct or piece of data tells us about, ironically, himself or herself—the person who has made a discovery, who lives (one hopes) with and by some larger vision of things.

I would like, for help, to call upon an American factory worker I've come to know these past years. The scientist (physician) in me has tried to contend with the illnesses that have afflicted him and his wife and children. The social scientist in me (a psychiatrist doing so-called "field work") has tried to comprehend how a man manages the various stresses imposed by a tough, demanding, exhausting assembly-line job. But there is in this person the stuff of the humanities, and I only hope I am sufficiently responsive to, respectful of, what he has to say:

> I feel good on the way to work. I leave the house early. It's the best time of the day. I see the sun come up. I do some thinking. Once I'm on the job, I have no time to think of anything; it's go, go, go—until I punch that card and leave. But on the road to my job I stop and ask myself questions. I mean, you want to have something to aim for; you want to believe in something. My oldest boy, he's starting college this September, the first one in our family to get that far. I told him—I said: get the best education you can, and it'll help you live better, and you'll get the respect of people; but don't forget to keep your common sense, and don't forget what life is all about.
>
> Sometimes, I think there's nothing to believe in, except the almighty dollar—and a little influence, that always helps. Sometimes, I see people behaving real rotten to other people, and I remember the wars in my lifetime, and I think of the troubles all over the world, and I think back to my father, and how he couldn't find a job when we were kids, and my mother being upset for him, and for us, and I remind myself of what a lousy life it still is for most of the people on this earth—well, I can get real low. But for all the trouble my family has had, and the world has had, I guess I'm lucky, because I don't stay down there in the dumps too long. I stop and say to myself that life may be a big mystery, like they tell you in church, but there's your family to hold on to, and the future your kids will have.

My little girl, she's eight years old; she asked me the other day if God pays attention to *every* person, and if He does, where does He get the time, and does He have the patience, or does He get tired? I told her it's not for me to know how God does His job, but I'll bet God thinks each grown up person should have a job, and should look after a few people, and try to pitch in—to help people who are in trouble. My wife and I have always tried to teach our children to be good and kind. I don't believe in church on Sunday and let the Devil run the show the rest of the week. I don't believe in talking to your children about God, and then teaching them to be cut-throat artists. I tell my children to stop themselves every few days, and look up at the sky, and listen to their conscience, and remember what they should believe in: give out as good as you want to get.

That was my father's philosophy of life. He didn't have a lot of material things to give, but he had himself—a big person he was; and he was always there to make us think twice before we stayed mean too long, and he was always there to make us realize the world doesn't circle around us. My wife says it's a real stroke of luck, to be alive, and living in this country, and not a lot of other places, and I'll tell you, people ought to stop and say yes, that's right, and yes, I'm here, and I'm going to give of myself, the best I know how—and maybe tomorrow, I'll find a way of being a better person; you tried to think about this life, and what you owe it, and you tried to get your kids to think about this life, too, and what they owe it.

His reflectiveness, his effort at detachment and introspection, in the midst of the press of everyday life, his struggle for decency and integrity and generosity, in the face of, inevitably, self-centeredness (the sin of pride), with all its attendant psychological mischief, ought qualify him, as much as anyone else in this land, as a *humanist*—a person who, often enough, draws upon and contributes to the tradition of the humanities. The humanities belong to no one kind of person; they are part of the lives of ordinary people, who have their own various ways of struggling for coherence, for a compelling faith, for social vision, for an ethical position, for a sense of historical perspective. The Foxfire tradition, now part of this nation's cultural life, has revealed how earnestly, seriously and conscientiously so-called "plain people" work to keep alive received values and ideals. When a north Georgia high school English teacher, Eliot Wigginton, started asking his students to leave the classroom upon occasion, he did so because he wanted to enrich learning, not dilute it.

Over a century ago, in Oxford, England, no less, Matthew Arnold urged novelists, poets and critics to become actively engaged in social, economic, and political affairs to bring their kind of sensibility to bear upon "the things of this world." He didn't have to send such a message to his contemporaries Charles Dickens or George Eliot; they kept their eyes carefully focused on the world, and through their fiction held up a mirror to an entire nation. George Eliot, as a young woman, was constantly letting herself learn from the rural English people she would later write about so knowingly. Here at home, William Faulkner made it his business to spend long hours with his fellow townspeople of Oxford, Mississippi—watching their habits and customs, hearing their stories, learning from them as well as sharing their news (and their bourbon). Where does the "real" Oxford end and the "made up" Yoknapatawpha begin? Of course, Faulkner was an imaginative artist, a man who made brilliant use of his mind's dreams and fantasies. But he came home every day from his "field-trips," they could be called, a rich man; he had been willing to be taught by his neighbors, and as a result had a lot to draw on as he sat at his desk writing.

The humanities demand that we heed the individual—each person worthy of respect, and no person unworthy of careful, patient regard. The humanities are blues and jazz; gospel songs and working songs; string quartettes and opera librettos; folk art and abstract impressionist art; the rich literary legacy of the nineteenth century Concord, or of the twentieth century South; the sayings and memories and rituals of countless millions of working people; the blunt, earthy self-justifications and avowals of desperate but determined migrant mothers; the wry, detached stories handed down on Indian reservations, in Eskimo villages, generation after generation; the cries of struggle and hope of Appalachia's hollow people, put into traditional ballads and bluegrass music; the photographs of Lewis Hine and Walker Evans and Russell Lee—ourselves presented to ourselves; the confident, qualified assertions of scholars; the frustrated, embittered social statements of ghetto teachers (or children), who at all costs want to get a grip on this puzzling, not always decent or fair world. The humanities are the essays and the novel, *Invisible Man,* of Ralph Ellison, so full of a writer's determination that race and poverty, still cruelly significant to a person's destiny, nevertheless are but partial statements—never enough to rob a person of his or her particularity; and the humanities are the essays and novels of Walker Percy, so full of wit and wisdom and shrewd moments of social analysis. The humanities are also the remarks of the New Orleans suburban people, the Louisiana bayou people Dr. Percy knows, learns from—remarks worthy indeed of being recorded, transcribed, added to an ("oral") literature; and too, the humanities are the musical sounds, the strong, spoken vernacular Ralph Ellison has in his writings taken pains to remind us of.

The National Endowment of the Humanities should, in its acts of encouragement, strive to do justice to the richness, the diversity of cultural life in a nation whose people are not, many of them, afraid to say what is on their minds as well as sing or draw or paint or write what is on their minds, and thereby, in sum, cast penetrating, knowing, critical judgments on what is happening in the world—judgments that ought to be put on the record, so to speak; that is, be acknowledged as part of America's cultural tradition.

THE SEACOAST OF BOHEMIA: TRUTH IN LITERATURE [5]

WALLACE A. BACON [6]

At a time when the humanities are being pushed aside in favor of science and career education, when wisdom is equated with what comes out of a computer, and when a study of the past is considered prosaic, Wallace A. Bacon, once more, reminds us of what literature has to offer. He sees it as a kind of communication that excites the understanding and imagination and develops sympathies, appreciation, and civility. Although he delivered his speech to teachers of speech communication his words convey thoughts that should inspire all who appreciate the liberal arts.

Bacon, president of the Speech Communication Association, spoke on December 2, 1977, to the members of his organization at their annual convention at the Sheraton Park Hotel, Washington, D.C. A teacher of the interpretation of literature in the School of Speech at Northwestern University, he was well known to his listeners and highly respected by them. They responded enthusiastically to what he had to say.

The address was carefully conceived and structured to advance the speaker's ideas. He introduced his theme with the following criticism of Shakespeare by Ben Jonson:

> In *The Winter's Tale,* he [Shakespeare] gave to Bohemia, the home of Polixenes and Florizel and the adopted land of Perdita, a seacoast. In Bohemia there is no sea near by some 100 miles. . . .

Bacon reinforced his theme and unified his speech by returning to *The Winter's Tale* criticism seven times and by alluding to other Shakespearean plays. In discussing Jonson, Bacon was able to establish his thesis that the geographical inaccuracies of Shakespeare are irrelevant to the great truths he communicates.

Teacher and lover of literature, Wallace A. Bacon defended

[5] Delivered at the general session of the national convention of the Speech Communication Association, Park-Sheraton Hotel, Washington, D.C., 10:30 A.M., December 2, 1977. Quoted by permission.

[6] For biographical note, see Appendix.

the humanities by contending that poetry, plays, and fiction communicate important messages to those who can grasp their essence. He added that:

> Literature makes possible the experiencing of the inexpressible. . . . Ultimately the great writer uncovers for us the deepest springs of our own experience, makes manifest in language and in symbolic action experiences we could never otherwise explore or endure, extends our horizons and stretches our spirit, gives wings to words and spurs to thoughts.

Carefully attuned to the nuances of language, Bacon gave full meaning to his words and evoked the proper feelings. In his quiet way he approached an eloquence that "the benighted rhetorician who still has some taste left for style" enjoys and admires.

That doughty classicist Ben Jonson was not one to bear lightly the failings of others. Much as he loved Shakespeare —if we take his commendatory verses in the 1623 folio to speak the truth—he was not above remarking in private, to William Drummond of Hawthornden, during the winter of 1618/19, that Shakespeare "wanted Art." He wanted besides, Jonson felt, an adequate knowledge of geography. In *The Winter's Tale,* he gave to Bohemia, the home of Polixenes and Florizel and the adopted land of Perdita, a seacoast. In Bohemia, said Jonson to Drummond, "there is no sea near by some 100 miles."

The view of the poet as liar goes back at least as far as Plato. The critics of literature—those for, as well as those against—have entered many a tilt and tournament over the matter. Sir Philip Sidney argued gravely that the poet affirms nothing and therefore never lies. ". . . though he recount things not true," says Sidney, "yet because he telleth them not for true, he lieth not. . . ." In support of his argument, Sidney says reasonably enough that men do not expect truth in the fables of Aesop—"for who thinks that Aesop writ it for actually true were well worthy to have his name chronicled among the beasts he writeth of." What Sidney might have said of Keats's boner in "On First Looking into Chapman's Homer," is perhaps another question, however. Many a student brought up on Keats will remember Cortes—not Balboa—as the discoverer of the Pacific Ocean, and Keats *did* expect to be believed.

Doubtless both Sidney and Jonson would have agreed that Keats was at fault. I don't know what Sidney would have said of the seacoast of Bohemia. But the issue they raise is no light one. What, after all, is the truth of literature?

I raise the question because it seems to me our own profession, on the whole, has not done terribly well by literature. *Serious* problems of communication, we are likely to feel, reside in real life—in the stresses and strains of politics and interpersonal relations, in the marketplace, on television, in small groups. Literature we leave, usually with relief, to interpretation and theatre, where it often looks to us like some embarrassing vestige from old concerns. Poems, plays, stories, novels—fictions, after all. Maybe not *lies*—that seems a bit harsh; but not really a serious concern of serious men and women. Or serious men, at least. Bohemia doesn't have a seacoast. Indeed, Shakespeare's Bohemia is like no Bohemia or land *or* sea.

I should argue in reply that literature is as much a fact of life as any other of the concerns to which scholars in communication nowadays address themselves. I should argue that from it I have probably learned more about communication between human beings than I have ever encountered in communication texts. I should argue that nowhere else have the codes through which and in which men and women interact been so sensitively and delicately explored, to the immense profit of readers. The poet *does* affirm, though to say this is not simply to contradict Sidney. Aesop's beasts, after all, are parts of the code, and they function affirmatively.

What Henry James once called "the old evangelical hostility" to fiction as wickedness is gone from today's world. *That* charge we willingly abandon. But the other charge, that fiction is "not serious," lingers—along, often, with the feeling which James attributed to many of its critics that fiction is often either "too frivolous to be edifying" or "too serious to be diverting."

James has the highest regard for his art, of course. And tion one may impose upon a novel in advance is that it be interesting. It must be free to find its way to that goal, and prescriptions in advance will only interfere with its progress. The ways by which the novel accomplishes its goal, says James, "are as various as the temperament of man, and they are successful in proportion as they reveal a particular mind, different from others. A novel is in its broadest definition a personal, a direct impression of life: that, to begin with, constitutes its value, which is greater or less according to the intensity of the impression. But there will be no intensity at all, and therefore no value, unless there is freedom to feel and say." "Experience," James goes on to say,

> is never limited, and it is never complete; it is an immense sensibility, a kind of huge spider-web of the finest silken threads suspended in the chamber of consciousness, and catching every airborne particle in its tissue. It is the very atmosphere of the mind; and when the mind is imaginative—much more when it happens to be that of a man of genius—it takes to itself the faintest hints of life, it converts the very pulses of the air into revelations. . . . The power to guess the unseen from the seen, to trace the implication of things, to judge the whole piece by the pattern, the condition of feeling life in general so completely that you are well on your way to knowing any particular corner of it—this cluster of gifts may almost be said to constitute experience. . . .

And then James gives what seems to me to be a splendid bit of advice: "Try to be one of the people on whom nothing is lost!" On most of us, I fear, much is lost. Literature can help us redress the balance.

James is doubtless right in arguing that the only obligahe is quite clear that not all literature lives up to his expectations. The quality of the mind of the writer matters greatly. Some of the ink that is spilled might better have remained in the bottle. (I must remember that that is *not* where ink is normally kept these days!) But at its best, literature does give us the mind in process. Nowhere else is human sensibility so sensitively displayed.

It is not my wish here to seem to be arguing for the study of literature as *opposed* to other forms of knowledge. Far from that. One of the virtues of our Association is, I think, the variety of its intentions, though as I said at the meeting of the Western Speech Communication Association some ten days ago I think there is a common *center* for those intentions. I *do* wish to argue for the study of literature as being near the core of our concerns, however—not peripheral, tangential, nor eccentric. Literature gives us, in its plentitude, a vast record of the failures and achievements of men and women in their attempts to come to grips with their lives.

I was about to say "an incredible record," but that reminds me that credibility is what we are to be talking about. Let's go back to the seacoast of Bohemia.

In his story of Leontes and Hermione and Perdita, Shakespeare stands near the end of his life as a playwright. *The Tempest* followed, and whatever of Shakespeare is in the play *Henry VIII*. But *The Winter's Tale* caps the exploration begun in *Pericles* and continued in *Cymbeline*. It is a story of parents and children, of loss and restoration, of jealousy and forgiveness. It is an intimate glimpse of the "chamber of consciousness" (to use James's phrase) of a great writer near the close of his career. And like all of the work of any great writer, it needs ultimately to be looked at in the context of that writer's total body of work. I can't, in the time I have, manage that kind of full look, but we can at least catch glimpses.

In the earlier romantic comedies, Shakespeare tackled the problems of love and romance. In play after play, he explored the elements which seem to make love work. Clearly he thought that women were better at it than men, and in large part because women seemed intuitively to grasp things which men had to learn by experience. That self-love, for example, makes true love difficult. That concern for others must often take precedence over concern for oneself. That wit and laughter help. That it is not always the brightest who are the best. That reason must sometimes bow to faith. That a knowledge of our own shortcomings ought to make us tolerant of others. That generosity and compassion are perhaps the greatest virtues to be found in life. That God does often indeed seem to help those who know best how to help themselves—and that to sit back and wait for God to act is sometimes to be unfair to heaven.

In the romantic comedies, love always leads to marriage; and in those plays, marriage seems to be the capstone of experience. The sun is always shining at the end of the romantic comedies, though sometimes through a little cloud or two. I do not mean to make the plays sound like homilies; they are not Sidney's sugar-coated pills. But whatever their absurdities (for they are, after all, comedies), they give us lives in operation in carefully articulated worlds, where the codes of communication are masterfully spelled out.

But in *The Winter's Tale* (a sad tale's best for winter, says the young boy Mamillius) the marriage of Leontes and Hermione comes upon terrible days; whatever lessons Leontes may have learned prior to marriage, he has new ones to learn now. That's the trouble with lessons; one forgets too easily what one has learned. Or learns that the problem has really never been understood at all. In the madness of his jealousy, King Leontes condemns his wife and sends his infant daughter Perdita to be exposed and left to die in the desert. Hermione, the Queen, is reported to have died; in actual fact, she goes into seclusion, where she remains some fifteen years. When her daughter Perdita is through a series of chances restored to Leontes, Hermione permits herself also to rejoin him, in a highly theatrical scene involving her spectacular stepping from art to life, and the parents and child are once again united.

At the moment of that final reunion, Shakespeare gives Hermione only one speech—7 lines out of a total of 155 in the scene—and it is addressed to her daughter, not to the husband whose jealousy caused the separation in the first place. But ask any class of students what goes on in the mind of Hermione as she comes back to life, and they will not lack words to describe her feelings. In a very early play, *The Two Gentlemen of Verona,* Shakespeare had another scene where one of his heroines stood speechless for 100 lines, but there it was impossible to imagine what on earth poor Silvia could have been thinking. She seemed to stand speechless because the playwright couldn't for the life of him imagine what she would have said. If she had said anything, she might indeed have taken the playwright to task for ineptness. But in *The Winter's Tale* Hermione doesn't speak because she doesn't need to—can't, because feelings are too deep and too full for words. She can forgive Leontes for what he has done, but she can never forget it, nor can he. The shadow of what he has done will hang over both of them for the remainder of their lives, and no words and no deeds can alter that fact. Still, life must go on. Perdita is home again, their child—and *she* is not to blame for what has happened; she must not be made to pay. And so the world begins again, renewing itself, doing its best to profit from past error. *The Winter's Tale* makes clear that the capstone of the romantic comedies, marriage, is only the beginning. Leontes needs to learn again—if he has ever learned it—the need for faith, for generosity, for compassion. Jealousy consumes its owner; love reaches out and sustains.

It cannot be said, with Sidney, that *The Winter's Tale* affirms nothing, though it *can* be said that Bohemia indeed has no seacoast. *The Winter's Tale* affirms, finally, within its own more *and* less than actual world, the worth of living. And it demonstrates, in its ultimate scene, the truth of Anthony Brandt's remark, in the current November issue of *The Atlantic,* that "works of art, *real* works of art, quite often take as their subject matter the distance between what people say and what they think and feel,"—and, I might add, what they often *do.*

But it's only a play. Historically, that "only" has been the refuge of those who find literature fun but useless, worth paying for but not worth heeding. And true enough, literature does in its mysterious way entertain us—"mysterious" because we often find ourselves responding raptly to things in themselves no way amusing—to Lear, to Macbeth, to Hamlet, to Othello. Pleasure is surely one of the uses of literature—joy is functional in our lives—but it is difficult to think of the death of Lear as pleasurable. We are moved rather, I think, by the fact that Lear's death is *true*. Not *actual,* but *true*. The actor playing Lear is not dying, but the Lear whom he acts is dying, dying, dying. The body fact is life; the body act is death. That enormous tension between the two states is real, is true. The general semanticist who said that the word *death* is meaningless because it cannot be understood until it is experienced, and then it cannot be explained, was talking through his hat. Literature makes possible the experiencing of the inexpressible. Hermione had no words for Leontes, but Shakespeare makes us understand what lay behind her silence. If students of communication are not interested in Shakespeare's achievement, I must feel great sorrow for them. We want our speech to be clear and direct, but—to quote Anthony Brandt once again, "one simplifies one's speech only by recognizing and coming to terms with its inescapable complexity. . . .

Ultimately, the great writer uncovers for us the deepest springs of our own experience, makes manifest in language and in symbolic action experiences we could never otherwise explore or endure, extends our horizons and stretches our spirits, gives wings to words and spurs to thoughts. The writer is a man who communes with the world in which he lives and communicates to us that unique act of communion in which he engages. There are great writers and there are not so great writers. There is nothing about writing which magically bestows virtue upon the writer. Some writing is not worth our time; some is worth all we can give to it. In literature, as in life, as in communication theory, as in rhetoric, as in the media, as in forensics, as in all the other activities to which we devote ourselves in this profession, there are values. Literature is no different from life in this respect; we must make choices in the things to which we devote our time—and sure, some of us in theatre and interpretation devote time to things perhaps not worth it. I don't value the inept writer any more than I value the inept anything else. But I value the great writer more than I value most others because from my own point of view he tells me most—and most effectively—about the way human beings speak and behave.

He does it through that marvellous instrument by way of which men and women share, with people whom they may never meet, the truths of experience. Much is to be said of non-verbal communication, and I am delighted that in this Association we are devoting much of our time to exploring its values, though we find ironically that in exploring it we usually *talk* about it. Much is to be said of the arts of painting and music and dance and sculpture, each of which has its own enduring human values to express. But surely it is true that our language and our speech offer us our strongest ties with our world, our uniquely human ties. To those who explore them most fully, we owe great thanks. Surely to be proud of being human—when we are able to be proud of that—ought to make us proud of those who speak most capably to and for us. The reduction of our language to the kind of jargon which infects the tongues of most of us too much of the time is no tribute to our capacities as men and women. If it seems worthwhile to be useful, to share, to respond, to inquire, to think, to feel—if it seems worthwhile to do these things, surely it should be worthwhile to increase, in whatever measure possible for each of us, the skill of the tongue which speaks and the language which lives upon that tongue. In this endeavor, poetry seems to me still the best teacher. There may be no seacoast in Bohemia, but Shakespeare's Bohemia has a seacoast. Ben Jonson was right, but Shakespeare is not wrong.

Two weeks ago, a white Boeing 707 bearing Egyptian President Anwar Sadat landed at Ben Gurion Airport in Tel Aviv. On whatever side of the Middle East argument one may stand, that moment must have seemed to almost anyone among the most moving moments of recent history, bearing as it did upon the hopes and fears of millions of people. It is interesting that in seeking to report it, in seeking to put into language the depth of the moment's feeling, *Time* magazine chose to cite a passage from literature. Whether one sees the Bible as revelation or as literature, it is clear enough that *Genesis* did not speak first in the English language in which *Time* cited it. Referring to a belief that the Edomites may be the forebears of today's Arabs, *Time* says:

> Some religious Jews even saw the Sadat-Begin meeting foreshadowed in the Torah text for the Sabbath . . . read at prayer services for that Saturday morning. It was a passage from *Genesis* describing the reconciliation of Jacob and his brother Esau, who fathered the Edomites. . . . A key passage from the reading: "Jacob lifted up his eyes and looked, and behold Esau came . . . and Esau ran to meet him, and embraced him, and fell on his neck, and kissed him, and they wept."

Literature lives through time, in time. It must be read both synchronically and diachronically. The *Time* report makes the most of the juncture of those two kinds of reading. For the moment, it brings the Bible to new life.

In the context of our own lives, this is what we always do with literature. Its truth is always in some part its truth to us. Men die, but their words may live. If we are interested, as we say, in communication, can we really believe that the living words of those long dead are of no *real* use to the living? That they are the toys of interpreters and actors and other perhaps well-meaning but light-headed individuals? Or of the benighted rhetorician who still has some taste left for style? We do rather badly by eloquence, in our Association.

Literature has plenty of truth in it, for us. In literature, language is used at its most human levels, in the exploration of the most human gestures. Surely to *this* kind of truth, too, we should encourage ourselves to listen. Let literature talk; let us listen. Even if it's to the sea rolling in on the seacoast of Bohemia.

THE FIGHT FOR EQUALITY, CONTINUED

"LET US JOIN HANDS, HEARTS AND MINDS"[1]

ROSALYN S. YALOW[2]

Rosalyn S. Yalow, the second woman to receive a Nobel Prize in physiology or medicine and the sixth woman to win such recognition in science, delivered a brief but eloquent speech to about 1,200 persons, 400 of whom were students at Stockholm University, at the traditional banquet in honor of the 1977 laureates.

After the formal ceremonies earlier in the day when the awards were bestowed, the winners were escorted to the City Hall for a festive occasion in a great room with high ceilings and great long tables. "One of the laureates always makes a speech to the students," reports Stig Ramel, president of the Nobel Foundation. Following the speech there was singing by a great chorus, and other musical entertainment, and a reception at which the king and queen of Sweden greeted the guests in a receiving line.

It was quite in keeping with the mood of the gathering that this distinguished scientist should comment on the problem of "social and professional discrimination," make a plea for understanding, and encourage her listeners to "join hands, hearts, and minds to work together." She is considered "a gifted and incisive lecturer," and serves as senior medical investigator at the Bronx Veterans Administration Hospital in New York City and research professor in the Department of Medicine at Mount Sinai School of Medicine, as well as adviser to important committees in medical science. She had received many honors prior to being awarded the Nobel Prize (*Science,* November 11, 1977, p 594).

Dr. Yalow has an expressive face and a well-modulated voice and speaks with assurance and persuasive directness.

Your Majesties, Your Royal Highnesses, Ladies, Gentlemen and you, the Students, who are the carriers of our hopes

[1] Delivered in Stockholm, Sweden, December 10, 1977, at the Nobel Foundation, 1977. Title supplied by editor. Quoted by permission of Dr. Yalow and the Nobel Foundation.

[2] For biographical note, see Appendix.

for the survival of the world and our dreams for its future. Tradition has ordained that one of the Laureates represent all of us in responding to your tribute. The choice of one among the several deemed truly and equally distinguished must indeed be difficult. Perhaps I have been selected for this privilege because there is certainly one way in which I am distinguishable from the others. This difference permits me to address myself first to a very special problem.

Among you Students of Stockholm and among other students, at least in the Western world, women are represented in reasonable proportion to their numbers in the community; yet among the scientists, scholars, and leaders of our world they are not. No objective testing has revealed such substantial differences in talent as to account for this discrepancy. The failure of women to have reached positions of leadership has been due in large part to social and professional discrimination. In the past, few women have tried and even fewer have succeeded. We still live in a world in which a significant fraction of people, including women, believe that a woman belongs and wants to belong exclusively in the home; that a woman should not aspire to achieve more than her male counterparts and particularly not more than her husband. Even now women with exceptional qualities for leadership sense from their parents, teachers, and peers that they must be harder-working, accomplish more and yet are less likely to receive appropriate rewards than are men. These are real problems which may never disappear or, at best, will change very slowly.

We cannot expect in the immediate future that all women who seek it will achieve full equality of opportunity. But if women are to start moving towards that goal, we must believe in ourselves or no one else will believe in us; we must match our aspirations with the competence, courage, and determination to succeed; and we must feel a personal responsibility to ease the path for those who come afterwards. The world cannot afford the loss of the talents of half its people if we are to solve the many problems which beset us.

If we are to have faith that mankind will survive and thrive on the face of the earth, we must believe that each succeeding generation will be wiser than its progenitors. We transmit to you, the next generation, the total sum of our knowledge. Yours is the responsibility to use it, add to it, and transmit it to your children.

A decade ago during the period of worldwide student uprisings there was deep concern that too many of our young people were so disillusioned as to feel that the world must be destroyed before it could be rebuilt. Even now, it is all too easy to be pessimistic if we consider our multiple problems: the possible depletion of resources faster than science can generate replacements or substitutes; hostilities between nations and between groups within nations which appear not to be resolvable; unemployment and vast inequalities among different races and different lands. Even as we envision and solve scientific problems—and put men on the moon—we appear ill-equipped to provide solutions for the social ills that beset us.

We bequeath to you, the next generation, our knowledge but also our problems. While we still live, let us join hands, hearts, and minds to work together for their solution so that your world will be better than ours and the world of your children even better.

FACES AND VOICES OF AMERICAN WOMEN [3]

LIZ CARPENTER [4]

The National Women's Conference held in Houston, Texas, on November 18, 19, 20, and 21, 1977, was attended by 1,950 delegates and an estimated 15,000 observers; 1,000 represented the press. The conference grew out of the observance of International Women's Year, proclaimed by the United Nations in 1975. Congress appropriated $5 million to finance meetings in the fifty states, as well as the national meeting in Houston.

Over 1,400 delegates (elected at 56 state and territorial meetings), over 180 alternates, and about 370 delegates at large appointed by an overseeing commission (*Update* 9, February 1978, National Commission on the Observance of International Women's Year) came from a cross-section of American life. Sixty-four percent were white; 17 percent, black; 8 percent, Hispanic; 3 percent, Asian-American; and 3 percent, American Indian. More than half came from the middle-income bracket, 14 percent from higher income ranges, and 23 percent from the lower-income bracket (*WEAL Washington Report,* December 1977). Pre-convention estimates indicated that about 80 percent of the delegates supported the conference national plan of action and 20 percent called themselves "pro-family delegates and opposed most of the plans" (Judy Klemesrud, New York *Times,* November 19, 1977). While the government-sponsored meeting was assembled at the Albert Thomas Convention Center in downtown Houston, five miles across town the Pro-Family, Pro-Life Coalition under the leadership of Phyllis Schlafly drew 11,000 to the Astro Arena (*Christian Science Monitor,* November 22, 1977).

Many prominent women participated in the conference and lent their support to it. In attendance were Lady Bird Johnson, Betty Ford, and Rosalynn Carter. Bella S. Abzug, former congresswoman from New York, presided. Representative Barbara Jordan of Texas, gave the keynote address. One of the delegates was Susan B. Anthony, grand-niece of the nineteenth century suffragist. Other speakers included Gloria Scott, national president, Girl Scouts of the USA; Esther Peterson, former special

[3] Delivered on November 19, 1977, 10 A.M., at the National Women's Conference, Houston, Texas. Quoted by permission.

[4] For biographical note, see Appendix.

assistant to the President for consumer affairs; Margaret Costanza, then assistant to the President for the Office of Public Liaison; Judge Shirley Hufstedler, US Circuit Judge from California; Coretta Scott King; and Margaret Mead.

In many ways the conference was reminiscent of the first women's rights convention in 1848 in Seneca Falls, New York, under the leadership of Elizabeth Cady Stanton and Lucretia Coffin Mott. Bella Abzug called the Houston conference "the most diverse meeting of American women ever held in this country."

Liz Carpenter, former Washington reporter and press secretary to Lady Bird Johnson and presently a moving force in the attempt to gain ratification of the Equal Rights Amendment, gave a stirring speech at the first plenary session shortly after 10 A.M. on November 19, 1977. Most of the delegates identified with the speaker because of her prominence in the fight for women's rights. Prior to her speech, the delegates had been greeted by the First Ladies. National IWY commissioners were introduced, as were the female members of Congress. The Seneca Falls Torch (carried in a 2,612-mile relay) was presented by poet Maya Angelou.

Carpenter's speech was an excellent reflection of the spirit of the meeting and brought her a standing ovation. Her repetition of the phrase "Not me" promoted rapport with her listeners and gave them an opportunity to participate, producing a unifying effect or what the critic Kenneth Burke has called consubstantiality or identification. The address, which stressed the diversity of the delegates was planned to answer charges by conservative opponents that the convention was not representative of American women in general. In many ways the speech resembled Martin Luther King, Jr.'s "I Have A Dream" speech. The student of speech composition will do well to study the effective use of parallel structure and repetition.

The eyes of the nation are on Texas today. As a native-born daughter, I assure you we like it that way!

Let the good news ring out! There is no energy shortage here in Houston—the Philadelphia of 1977. Here is a supply of America's greatest untapped energy resource—set aside for 201 years—misused and unused (a fuel that comes with brains)—the women of America.

This year something quite wonderful happened. Every woman living under the American flag had a chance to attend a meeting, vote her mind, and send a delegation here to this national summit of women.

So here we are. The faces and voices ignored and silenced too often by the decision-makers. The President of the United States and the Congress have asked us to assess our needs, assert our worth, and set our goals for filling the legislative gaps.

I thought they'd never ask!

Unafraid, uninhibited, let us speak to the future well-being of America.

Let us write our report clearly—not for just one segment of us, but for all. Let us write it firmly so there is no future doubt about it as we move our needs from our homes onto the desks of every lawmaker in America for action.

For, Mr. President, members of Congress, until the women of the United States are full equal operating citizens, your cry for human rights around this globe will have a very hollow ring.

Who are "We the people" gathered here in Houston? We are the female people left out in Philadelphia, and the irony—the real irony—is that there would have been no America without us. So we are here to stake our claim on its past and its future.

We have been necessary to it from the beginning. It took a woman—Queen Isabella—to have the faith to send Columbus to discover America. She heard his pleas and put up the money for the voyage.

We crossed the Atlantic to Boston and Jamestown. Again, it took a woman to remember to bring along a printing press. We weren't included in Philadelphia to write the founding documents. We printed them! The only name of a woman on the American Constitution is Mary Katherine Goddard, Baltimore printer.

As America moved westward, it was a woman—Sacagawea—the Indian maiden who led Lewis and Clark to the Pacific. Can't you see her now? "Look, palefaces—Big Water—Pacific!"

Across the open plains we trudged every weary foot of it, embraced the majesty of the American Rockies, wrote about it, sang songs about it, helped build the log cabins, light the lanterns of the frontier. It was a lonely land, an empty land and we peopled it. Yes, we made the people (and sometimes we overdid that). We founded the churches and Sunday schools, and with homespun simplicity nurtured the population with faith and spirit.

Once settled, we have seen our own dreams sometimes shattered, often shortchanged, doors closed, or half closed by insecure men and women fearful of a world of equality.

Are we so dangerous? So alien to this land we have founded? Are we so threatening? So "forward" and "brash" and "pushy" to ask for fairness.

We mothered this nation. Are we to be penalized for it forever? We have no intention of abandoning our role as nurturer or wife, mother, responsible sisters, loving daughters, tax-paying citizens. Some of us are homemakers, some breadwinners, most women are both.

I've spent most of my life being both. Enjoyed both. I know the warmth of a baby's laughter and as a journalist, the satisfaction of a newspaper by-line. I know the panic and loneliness of widowhood. Many in this room do—or will.

Are we to be forever shackled by "the unending audacity of elected men?"

We are the map of America. Some of us think the country's moving too slowly. Some fear it will move too fast. Our roots are privileged and they are humble. So here we are inside this hall and out—women of many faces and voices. We are not all as passionate as Bella, as perceptive and photogenic as Gloria, as judicious as Judge Shirley Hufstedler, as futuristic as Betty Friedan, as impish as Amy or mellow as Miss Lillian, as caring as Rosalynn, dedicated as Lady Bird, gentle as Pat Nixon, or courageous as Betty Ford.

But something of all of them is in all of us. We are not

look-alikes, and think-alikes, and God forbid that we ever will be.

Look at us. Who are we today?

Some homemakers—some breadwinners—some both. How many homemakers are here? All homemakers—hold up your hands.

Any breadwinners out there? All you people who earn a salary—big or small—hold up your hands.

We come from all ages. Let's see how many are under thirty? How many are somewhere between forty and death?

Who else are we? We are voters—since 1920—and there was a lot of "brouhaha" about that! We are volunteers and rising new voices at City Hall and the state capitals.

We are in public office by election and appointment! Republicans, Democrats, independents . . . nothing.

Let's see how many public [office] holders out there. Hold up your hands.

Who are we delegates? We are young and old.

Sixteen-year-old Dorothy Arceneaux of Houma, Louisiana. Honor student, Girl Scout leader, member of the school band. *Would you deny this young girl the right to equality of education and opportunity?* Not me!

Eighty-five-year-old Clara M. Beyer of Washington, D.C., retired government worker of sixty years—protégée of Justice Frankfurter, teacher at Bryn Mawr College, one of the handful of valiant women who with Eleanor Roosevelt and Florence Kelley pushed the reform of child labor, mother of 3 sons and 12 grandchildren. *Would you deny this senior citizen mother the social security rights due her—or deny women like her their inheritance rights?* Not me!

Twenty-four-year-old Mariko Tse—delegate from California, actress, leader in Chinese Women in Action. At the age of eight, she was a world traveler, standing before a judge to get her citizenship, now a leader in Upwardbound programs with blacks, chicanas, Indians, and the American Chinese. She came to meet the Asian women in all the delegations. "That gives me a terrific thrill—to see them moving ahead." She said. *Would you deny this ethnic American—or any other ethnic American women—the rights of equality under the law?* Not me!

Politically active wives of governors like delegate Helen Millikin of Michigan and Sharon Percy Rockefeller of West Virginia who do their volunteerism in environment and the crafts of Appalachia. *Would you deny these women and many like them—housewives and mothers—the right to do magnificent things for their communities and their states? Could their communities survive without their volunteer time?* Not me!

Vida Haukass, trial judge from Wind River Reservation in Fort Washaske, Wyoming, her Indian name is Sinopahki. "I have come to hear what everybody else thinks." *Would you deny this native American any right from the country which was her land long before it was ours?* Not me?

The delegate from Kansas—Sister Mary Agnes Drees—director of continuing education at Marymount College—a member of the Sisters of St. Joseph and the network lobby of Catholic sisters working for social justice. "The Sisters of St. Joseph were always in the vanguard of change on the frontier. We are still there working in our precincts, active politically in City Hall," she returns sixty percent of her salary to support Marymount College where she teaches. *Would you deny this religious woman—or any religious woman of any creed a voice or the right to move ahead in their religious group?* Not me!

The delegate from Illinois—Marge Jinrich—fourteen years with the United Auto Workers, Local 954 of Region IV. She helps support her semi-invalid husband and five children on a paycheck of $8,500. "My husband and my children believe like I do—that things aren't moving fast enough for women in the legislature at Springfield or in the unions. There's too much foot-dragging. Something needs to happen. I want to help make it happen." *Would you deny this mother and wife the right to attempt to move the unions forward in the matter of equality of opportunity for women?* Not me!

Delegate at large from Georgia—Mrs. Jack Carter—Judy, young homemaker, and mother of a two-year-old son and baby-sitter for his five friends quite frequently, as you can detect over the phone.

We are Margie Flores, of El Paso, Texas, chair of the Chicano Women's Caucus—mother of four and now back in school herself studying elementary education so she can teach. "I want women to learn they can work together with the commonality that binds us together." *Would you deny this woman and the thousands like her their full rights as citizens of this great nation?* Not me!

The delegate from Minnesota—farm woman Mary Ann Brueschoffe, who runs her own poultry farm on Route 2 near Watkins. She was butchering ducks when I called. While her husband raises pigs, cattle and sheep, she just fell into raising 3,000 broilers, ducks, and geese each year because "We like good old fashioned food that's uncontaminated. Everyone else did too and it helps pay the college tuition of three of four children." Why did she want to come? "I demand of our society that attitudes be the same toward the sexes and the races. It is inconceivable to me in a democracy that we cause anyone pain because of preconceived notions about the way people should feel toward one another." *Would you keep this woman out of business because she couldn't get equal credit to run a business—or un-*

fair taxes that prevent her from deductions that are allowable to her counterparts? Not me!

The delegate from New York—Georgia McMurray, long-time leader in movements for civil rights and the disabled—brings head and heart to New York's community services. *Woud you deny this and any of the millions of black women the right to go as far as their dreams and magnificent talents can take them.* Not me!

That's who we are—this great women's movement. Progress always begins with a movement. But all movements of people become movements of individuals and that is where we are today, establishing a belief in ourselves, gaining the courage to walk in the sunshine of our own souls.

That is the final greatness a nation derives from the movements of its times. The gift of individual courage in people to be their own selves and speak their own thoughts.

America, look at us! Listen to us. Have faith in us. Help us. Love us as we loved you.

CELEBRATING HUBERT H. HUMPHREY

I AM OPTIMISTIC ABOUT AMERICA[1]

HUBERT H. HUMPHREY[2]

Generally the Senate of the United States grinds away tediously on its routine business. Even major speeches seldom attract more than scant or spasmodic attendance. But the session, October 22, 1977, was different. Senators and their staff members crowded the floor, and spectators filled the galleries. Regular business ceased. The senators welcomed back one of their favorite colleagues—Senator and former Vice President Hubert H. Humphrey, who had been absent for two months suffering with terminal cancer. For six minutes the Minnesotan shook hands and greeted his fellow senators on both sides of the aisle, hugging some—clerks, parliamentarians, and even the pages (Stephen E. Nordlinger, Baltimore *Sun,* October 26, 1977).

Robert C. Byrd (Democrat, West Virginia), the majority leader; Howard H. Baker, Jr. (Republican, Tennessee), the minority leader; and Wendell R. Anderson (Democrat, Minnesota) delivered speeches of welcome (*Congressional Record,* October 25, 1977, p S17677-9). One reporter called it "a dramatic moment unprecedented in the memory of veteran Senate observers" (James R. Dickerson, Washington *Star,* October 26, 1977).

Gaunt from his recent illness, Humphrey responded with an emotional and extemporaneous speech. Known for his loquaciousness, he showed his usual enthusiasm and optimism. In a light-hearted mood, he injected self-deprecating humor in his speech, with graciousness and good taste. Through his brief words he reflected his closeness to his fellow senators, his buoyancy, and his deep commitment to the Senate.

This speech was not one of Humphrey's best ones, but it demonstrated that he was still a skillful communicator who understood how to adapt his remarks to an occasion deeply charged with emotion.

[1] Delivered on the floor of the US Senate, October 22, 1977. Title supplied by editor. Quoted by permission.

[2] For biographical note, see Appendix.

My esteemed colleagues, may I say that the distinguished minority leader has an unusual insight into my weakness and my personality. My good friend, Senator Bumpers, sitting alongside of me here said, "This is just a little too much, isn't it, Hubert?" And I said: "Hush. I like it." [Laughter.]

After all, I remember Abourezk and Metzenbaum going here for days. I see no reason that I should not come back and join in. I did not have a chance to really participate. I was frustrated beyond no end.

Russell Long just thanked me. He said: "There is nothing like having Hubert away." [Laughter.]

Gentleman, most of you know me as a sentimental man, and that I am. Today is a very special day in my life, not only because I feel strong enough to come to this historic Chamber, back to the US Senate, the greatest parliamentary body in the world, but more significantly because of the genuine friendship and warmth that has been exhibited here today by my colleagues. The greatest gift in life is the gift of friendship, and I have received it. And the greatest healing therapy is friendship and love, and over this land I have sensed it. Doctors, chemicals, radiation, pills, nurses, therapists, are all very, very helpful, but without faith in yourself and in your own ability to overcome your difficulties, faith in divine providence and without the friendship and the kindness and the generosity of friends, there is no healing. I know that.

I have been going through a pretty rough struggle. But one of my doctors back home said: "Hubert, we have done about as much for you as we can for a while. Why don't you go back to Washington where you want to be, where your colleagues in the Senate are and where you can be with your friends, those whom you love so much?" And I said: "Doctor, that is good advice."

Only once before had I ever wished a doctor to give me advice of a similar nature, namely, take a long vacation, and I followed this advice. I waited, however, because I am a frugal man, until I could get a free ride. [Applause.]

Some of you were at that dinner to which my good and dear friend and esteemed colleague, Senator Wendell Anderson, referred. They tell me it was a truly delightful occasion. I wanted everybody to have fun. I said then that the only reason I did not come to that dinner was not because I was physically unable, but because I got an invitation from the President, through the good offices of my lobbyist in the White House, the Vice President, my special friend, to come back on Air Force One.

Well, for at least twenty years I have been trying to get on Air Force One. [Laughter.] I realize it was not a prolonged experience, but just the thought of it, the vibrations, gave me new hope and new strength.

On Sunday, our President, Jimmy Carter, stopped in the Twin Cities, picked up me and Mrs. Humphrey, and we came back to Washington.

It was a beautiful trip. I had a chance to visit with President Carter and to express to him some of my concerns and my hopes.

I want to put it just this way: I have been known in my life to be an optimist, some people say a foolish optimist, and I suppose at times I have ignored reality and had more than the usual degree of optimism. But I said to the critics that I am optimistic about America, and that I rebuke their cynicism.

The reason I do is because history is on my side. We have come a long way in this country. More people today are enjoying more of what we call, at least in the material sense, the good things of life in every form. We have made fantastic strides in science, technology, and engineering. Our agriculture is the wonder of the world. But, most of all, we are a heterogeneous population, and we are trying to demonstrate to the world what is the great moral message of the Old and New Testaments; namely, that people can live together in peace and in understanding because really that is the challenge, that is what peace is all about.

It is not a question of whether we pile up more wealth; it is a question of whether or not we can live together, different races, different creeds, different cultures, different areas, not as a homogeneous people but rather in the pluralistic society where we respect each other, hopefully try to understand each other, and then have a common bond of devotion to the Republic.

I have a blind devotion to the Senate, which represents the Republic. This is a great institution, and all of us want to add to it by our conduct, by our efforts.

You have been very flattering toward me. I want you to know that I am old enough and sufficiently wise enough at this stage of my life to know that all you have said is not exactly according to facts. [Laughter.] But I also want you to know that I am sufficiently fragile and weak as to want to believe every single word you have said. [Laughter and applause.]

To the majority leader, I thank you once again. The bonds of the friendship that have grown between us, particularly this past year, are truly beautiful, and I want to be of help wherever I can, and that is true of my colleagues.

What a wonderful place this is, where we can argue, fight, have different points of view, and still have a great respect for one another and, many times, deep affection.

I must not mention more names because there are so many here who have meant so much to me, but I just want you to know that when it comes to the Senate and to what this body means, it is not Democrat or Republican. It is "citizen," which I consider to be the highest honor that can be paid to any person in the world, higher than emperor or king or prince, to be citizen of the United States and then, as a citizen, to be elected and selected by our own constituency to represent the citizenry in this body. What a great honor.

May the Good Lord give each of us the strength to never in any way besmirch that honor, but in every day of our lives, as we see what we believe to be the truth, as we dedicate ourselves to what we believe to be best for our country, even though we may disagree, let us conduct ourselves in a manner that future historians will say, "These were good people. They were good men. They were good representatives, at a time when the nation needed them." And our nation does need us now.

Now, my plea to us is, in the words of Isaiah, as a former President used to say—and I mean it very sincerely—come, let us reason together. There are no problems between the different points of view in this body that cannot be reconciled, if we are willing to give a little and to share a little and not expect it all to be our way. Who is there who has such wisdom that he knows what he says is right? I think we have to give some credence to the fact that majority rule, which requires the building of an understanding and the sharing, at times the compromising, is the best of all forms of rule.

Well, I got wound up. I did not intend to be that long, but that has been the story of my life. You would want me to be natural. Thank you very much. Thank you very, very much.

[Prolonged applause, Senators and guests rising.]

A TRIBUTE TO THE MAN OF THE PEOPLE[3]

JOSEPH CALIFANO, JR.[4]

Between October 25, when he returned to the Senate, and his death on January 13, 1978, many tributes were paid to Hubert H. Humphrey. One of the most eloquent was the speech that Joseph Califano, Jr., secretary of the Department of Health, Education, and Welfare, made at the dedication of the Hubert H. Humphrey HEW Building, November 1, 1977.

The brief speech highlighted the legislative accomplishments of the Minnesota Democrat. It is an excellent tribute and most fitting for dedication. Its power grows out of the specific details and the enumeration of the programs for which Humphrey worked. The speaker wisely let the quotation from Teilhard de Chardin climax his development. Too many times a speaker on an occasion such as this one turns to excessive figurative language for effect, hence becoming maudlin and embarrassing. Califano exercised good judgment and taste.

Now and then in America someone comes along whose life and career remind us not just how good he is, but of how good we can be.

For our generation and for me personally, because I have been privileged to know Senator Humphrey for so long and so intimately, Hubert Humphrey is that person. He has earned our respect and won our love. Not simply for what he has done but for what he has been, and for all that he has summoned us to be.

Today we honor him in an especially fitting way. Today, the department of the people pays tribute to the man of the people. From this day forward this building which for millions of Americans is the headquarters of health and hope will bear the name of the man who symbolizes this government's capacity to offer help and hope.

[3] Delivered at the dedication of the Hubert H. Humphrey Health, Education, and Welfare Building, November 1, 1977.

[4] For biographical note, see Appendix.

In this building we administer programs that touch the lives of the most vulnerable in America. Programs to feed the hungry, to help the poor, to care for the sick, to rehabilitate the handicapped, to teach the young, to enrich the life for the old and to end discrimination.

How appropriate that our efforts shall be carried on under the name of the man who fathered so many of these programs. It is Hubert Humphrey who proposed in 1949 a national program of medical care for the aged under the Social Security System, legislation that sixteen years later became Medicare.

It is Hubert Humphrey who before almost anyone else fought for legislation forbidding discrimination against the blacks, the ethnics, the aged and the handicapped. It is Hubert Humphrey who guided to passage hopeful programs like Headstart. Dozens of programs from wider Social Security coverage, to federal scholarships to Biomedical Research, owe their present strength and their existence to Hubert Humphrey's leadership as architect, sponsor, and advocate.

And dozens more that do not yet exist like National Health Insurance, will exist because of the early vision and leadership of Hubert Humphrey.

For Hubert Humphrey is not only a leader in America, he is a prophet. A prophet lifting our lives continually from what we have achieved to what we must achieve. From the road behind us to the road ahead.

Today, Senator Humphrey, we do not honor you so much as you honor us by lending your name, your inspiration and your example to the work we do here.

There are some words, Senator, of the Jesuit philosopher Teilhard de Chardin that capture well the energy and the joy that enrich your life.

Teilhard wrote:

"Someday after mastering the winds, the waves, the tides and gravity we shall harness for God the energies of love, and then for the second time in the history of the world man will have discovered fire."

It is your achievement, Senator, to harness in a remarkable career those energies of love to generate warmth and light for millions of your countrymen. It means a great deal for all of us and I can't tell you how much it means to me personally to be secretary at this moment. It gives me a great deal of pleasure to call upon someone else who is a special friend of this department and a man I have admired for many years and a special friend of mine, your colleague and protégé from Minnesota, a man in whose own achievements, your spirit, the spirit and example of Hubert Humphrey can be seen, your friend and successor in two high national offices, the Vice President of the United States.

MY GOOD FRIEND HUBERT HUMPHREY[5]

JIMMY CARTER[6]

During the brief return of Hubert H. Humphrey to his Senate duties, the new Health, Education, and Welfare Building was dedicated to him and named in his honor (see preceding speech by Joseph Califano, Jr.). On December 2, 1977, a dinner was held in the International Ballroom at the Washington Hilton Hotel to launch a $20 million subscription for the Hubert Humphrey Institute of Public Affairs at the University of Minnesota (to be dedicated in July 1978). The thousand-dollar-a-plate dinner drew two thousand people, who were entertained by a notable cast of popular actors and singers. All honored the Minnesota senator "not as a senator and not as a leader of the Democratic Party, but as an American symbol of the great heart and the good spirit" (Washington *Post,* December 3, 1977).

At this dinner President Carter, "who is rarely available for jocular after-dinner speeches at testimonial rituals, proved an enormous hit" (John J. Carmody, Washington *Post,* December 3, 1977). He devoted his speech to examples of how Senator Humphrey had touched his life—"a few brief instances that occurred . . . long before I had any dreams of coming to Washington myself." He related his stories well, as he reinforced the favorable image of the Minnesota senator. Perhaps the President may make his best use of his informal style on occasions like this one, coming across as a down-to-earth, warm, friendly man.

Early this week, my good friend Charles Kirbo came to Washington. He said he was getting very worried about me, that he couldn't understand how every time he saw me, I looked older and older and Senator Humphrey looked younger and younger.

He said Senator Humphrey always has a smile on his face. He said, "Jimmy, your smile is gone." [*Laughter.*] He said, "Your hair is turning gray; his has gotten curly." I

[5] Delivered at a dinner in honor of Hubert H. Humphrey, International Ballroom, Washington Hilton Hotel, December 2, 1977.

[6] For biographical note, see Appendix.

said, "Well, the difference is that Senator Humphrey has been here long enough in Washington to know how to handle the political scene and I haven't learned yet."

Last summer, just as the Senate was beginning its long two-month filibuster, Senator Humphrey went back to Minnesota for a vacation. And at the end of the vacation, when he got ready to come back, again being very conversant with political ways, he called me up and said, "Mr. President, I'd like to come back to Washington." I said, "Well, Senator Humphrey, we're glad to have you." He said, "Yes, but I need a ride." [*Laughter.*] And I said, "Well, that's fine. Maybe I could send the Vice President out to pick you up." He said, "Well, I've never ridden in Air Force One."

So, I went to the west coast and came back via Minnesota and picked him up. But first I said, "Well, why is it you want to come back?" He said, "I think if I come back, I can get the Congress straightened out." He said, "I guarantee you, if you give me a ride back to Washington, I'll have the energy package passed in a week." [*Laughter.*]

He is a man who has touched my life and that of my family, as I'm sure he's touched almost everyone here in a strange and very delightful way. And I'm going to tell you just a few brief instances that occurred, actually, long before I had any dreams of coming to Washington myself.

The first time I heard about Senator Humphrey was when I was in the Navy, and he made a famous speech at the Democratic National Convention. He was quite well-known in Georgia. I don't think anyone else has kept more Georgia politicians from seeing the end of a Democratic Convention than Senator Humphrey has, because it got so that every time he walked in, they walked out and came back home. [*Laughter.*]

So, in 1964, when he became the vice-presidential candidate, in Georgia, it wasn't a very popular thing to be for the Johnson-Humphrey slate. My mother, Lillian, ran the Sumter County Johnson-Humphrey headquarters. And I could always tell when my mother was coming down the road, because she was in a brand new automobile with the windows broken out, the radio antenna tied in a knot, and the car painted with soap. [*Laughter.*]

In that campaign, Hubert and Muriel came down to south Georgia to Moultrie for a Democratic rally. And because of my mother's loyalty, she was given the honor of picking up Muriel at the airport. And Rosalynn and my mother and Muriel and my sister Gloria went down to Moultrie to attend the rally. Senator Humphrey made a speech, and they had a women's reception for Muriel. And they were riding around that south Georgia town getting ready for the reception. Everybody in town was very excited. And as Muriel approached the site, she said, "Are any black women invited to the reception?"

For a long time no one spoke, and finally my sister said, "I don't know." She knew quite well that they weren't. And Muriel said, "I'm not going in." So, they stopped the car, and my sister Gloria went inside to check and let the hostess know that Muriel was not coming to the reception. But in a few minutes, Gloria came back and said, "Mrs. Humphrey, it's okay." So, she went in and, sure enough, there were several black ladies there at the reception. And Muriel never knew until now that the maids just took off their aprons for the occasion. [*Laughter.*] But that was the first integrated reception in south Georgia, Muriel, and you are responsible for it.

Ten or eleven years ago, when I was not in political office at all, Senator Humphrey was Vice President. He had been to Europe on a long, tedious, very successful trip. And he came down to Atlanta, Georgia, to visit in the home of a friend named Marvin Shube. And I was invited there to meet him, which was a great honor for me. I have never yet met a Democratic President, and he was the only Democratic Vice President I had ever met. And I stood there knowing that he was very weary because he had just returned from Europe. But he answered the eager questions of those Georgia friends until quite late in the morning, about two o'clock. And he was very well briefed, because when I walked in the room, he said, "Young man, I understand that your mother is in the Peace Corps in India."

And I said, "Yes, sir, that's right." He said, "Well, I've been very interested in the Peace Corps. The idea originally came from me, and I've been proud to see it put into effect." He said, "Where's your mother?" And I said, "She's near Bombay." He said, "How's she getting along?" I said, "Well, she's quite lonely, sir. She's been there about six months, and she's not seen anybody, even the Peace Corps officials. She's in a little town called Vikhroli."

About a month later, I got a letter from my mother. She was in her room one evening, and the head of the Peace Corps in India had driven up to the little town of Vikhroli. He came in and asked my mother if she needed anything. She said, no, she was getting along quite well, but she would like to go over to Bombay. He said, "Well, can I take you in shopping, Mrs. Carter?" She said, "Yes, I'd like that." So, they went in, and he bought her a very fine supper and brought her back to Vikhroli. When he got out, he handed her a fifth of very good bourbon. [*Laughter.*] And he turned around to get in the car to leave, and he finally turned back to her and said, "By the way, Miss Lillian, who in the hell are you, anyway?" [*Laughter.*] And that's a true story. It was not until later that my mother knew who she was. [*Laughter.*] She was a friend of Hubert Humphrey.

And, of course, the next time he crossed my path was in 1968 when he was our nominee for President. And all of us in this room went through that year of tragedy together when he was not elected to be the leader of our country. And I think he felt then an urging to be loyal to his President and, unfortunately, many people were not that loyal to him. And his loss was our nation's even greater loss in 1968.

The next time I saw him was when I was governor. He came to our home in 1972. All the candidates just happened to stop by to see me that year, and my daughter, Amy, was about four years old. And most of the ones who would come into the mansion—she stayed away from them, having an early aversion to politicians. But when Senator Humphrey came in, she loved him instantly.

And I'll never forget sitting in the front presidential suite of the Georgia governor's mansion, a very beautiful room, trying to talk to Senator Humphrey. Amy came in eating a soft brownie, and she climbed up on his lap without any timidity at all. In a very natural way, he put his arm around her as though she was his own grandchild. And I'll always remember Senator Humphrey sitting there talking to me about politics and about the campaign, smiling often, with brownie all over his face. [*Laughter.*] And each time he frowned, brownie crumbs fell to the floor. And Amy loved him then and has loved him ever since. But I think she recognized in him the qualities that have aroused the love of so many people.

And then, of course, last year all I could hear everywhere I went when I said, "Would you help me become President?" almost invariably they would say, "Well, my first preference is Hubert Humphrey. If he doesn't run, I'll support you." And there again, I learned on a nationwide basis the relationship between Senator Humphrey and the people of this country.

But I think the most deep impression I have of my good friend Hubert Humphrey is since I've been President. I've seen him in the Oval Office early in the morning. I've seen him in meetings with other congressional leaders. I've called him on the phone when I was in trouble. I've gotten his quiet and private and sound advice. And I've come to recognize that all the attributes that I love about America are resident in him. And I'm proud to be the President of a nation that loves a man like Hubert Humphrey and is loved so deeply by him.

Thank you very much.

A TIME TO CELEBRATE LIFE[7]

WALTER F. MONDALE[8]

Hubert H. Humphrey was given a state funeral befitting a former Vice President of the United States and a prominent senator. After his death at his home in Waverly, Minnesota, January 13, 1978, his remains were flown aboard Air Force One, the presidential plane, for a service in the Capitol Rotunda in Washington, D.C. The memorial service was held January 15, at 11 A.M., before a distinguished audience of 1,500, including President Carter and former Presidents Ford and Nixon (the latter's first return to Washington since his resignation August 9, 1974). Also present were several persons who had sought the presidency—including Senator Edmund Muskie of Maine, Senator Barry Goldwater of Arizona, and former Senator Eugene McCarthy—and Lady Bird Johnson. Eulogies were delivered by President Carter and Vice President Walter F. Mondale. Following the service, the Rotunda was opened, and 55,000 citizens paid their respects to the man affectionately known as "the Happy Warrior."

At a second service at the Hope Presbyterian Church in St. Paul at 2:30 P.M. on January 16, Carter and Mondale again delivered eulogies. Any of the four eulogies, the two by President Carter and two by Vice President Mondale, would be suitable for inclusion in this volume. However, the one Mondale delivered in Washington is included here because it reflected the close ties between the Vice President and his long-time mentor.

"That this be a time to celebrate life and the future, not to mourn the past and his death." With these words Vice President Walter F. Mondale explained Humphrey's "last great wish" regarding his funeral. Mondale's press secretary, Albert Eisele, affirmed that the following account of the speech preparation is factual (letter to editor, April 7, 1978):

> The day before the Sunday service at the Capitol, Mondale met in his home with his press secretary, Al Eisele, and Norman Sherman, Humphrey's former press secretary and the man who helped write the senator's auto-

[7] Delivered in the Rotunda of Capitol, Washington, D.C., at 11 A.M., January 15, 1978.

[8] For biographical note, see Appendix.

> biography. At one point Mondale opened a copy of Shakespeare's *Henry V* . . . and read a passage that he said expressed how he felt about Humphrey. They, Eisele and Sherman, worked on a draft, with Sherman staying up most of the night applying finishing touches. Mondale contributed the Shakespeare and the dramatic closing: "He taught us all how to hope and how to love, how to win and how to lose, he taught us how to live, and finally he taught us how to die" (Rudy Maxa, "People," Washington *Post,* January 15, 1978).

The Vice President's tribute could not be called an eloquent eulogy. It was the personal statement of a close friend very deeply involved in the loss and the occasion. In language and sentiment, the speech did not compare with Adlai Stevenson's tribute to Winston Churchill (REPRESENTATIVE AMERICAN SPEECHES: 1964-1965, p 103-11) or Dean Rusk's address in memory of Lyndon Johnson (REPRESENTATIVE AMERICAN SPEECHES: 1972-1973, p 132-7). But no one will question its moving quality and its sincerity. As a speech it tells the reader much about Hubert H. Humphrey.

Dear Muriel, the Humphrey family and guests:

There is a natural impulse at a time like this to dwell on the many accomplishments of Hubert Humphrey's remarkable life, by listing a catalogue of past events as though there were some way to quantify what he was all about. But I don't want to do that because Hubert didn't want it and neither does Muriel. Even though this is one of the saddest moments of my life and I feel as great a loss as I have ever known, we must remind ourselves of Hubert's last great wish:

That this be a time to celebrate life and the future, not to mourn the past and his death. I hope you will forgive me if I don't entirely succeed in looking forward and not backward. Because I must for a moment. Two days ago as I flew back from the west over the land that Hubert loved to this city that he loved, I thought back over his life and its meaning and I tried to understand what it was about this unique person that made him such an uplifting symbol of hope and joy for all people. And I thought of the letter that he wrote to Muriel forty years ago when he first visited Washington.

He said in that letter:

> Maybe I seem foolish to have such vain hopes and plans, but Bucky, I can see how some day, if you and I just apply ourselves and make up our minds to work for bigger things, how we can some day live here in Washington and probably be in government, politics or service. I intend to set my aim at Congress.

Hubert was wrong only in thinking that his hopes and plans might be in vain. They were not, as we all know. Not only did he succeed with his beloved wife at his side, he succeeded gloriously and beyond even his most optimistic dreams.

Hubert will be remembered by all of us who served with him as one of the greatest legislators in our history. He will be remembered as one of the most loved men of his times. And even though he failed to realize his greatest goal, he achieved something much more rare and valuable than the nation's highest office. He became his country's conscience.

Today the love that flows from everywhere enveloping Hubert flows also to you, Muriel, and the presence today here, where America bids farewell to her heroes, of President and Mrs. Carter, of former Presidents Ford and Nixon, and your special friend and former first lady, Mrs. Johnson, attest to the love and the respect that the nation holds for both of you. That letter to Bucky, his Muriel, also noted three principles by which Hubert defined his life: work, determination and high goals. They were a part of his life's pattern when I first met him thirty-one years ago. I was only eighteen, fresh out of high school, and he was the mayor of Minneapolis. He had then all the other sparkling qualities he maintained throughout his life: boundless good humor, endless optimism and hope, infinite interests, intense concern for people and their problems, compassion without being patronizing, energy beyond belief, and a spirit so filled with love there was no room for hate or bitterness.

He was simply incredible. When he said that life was not meant to be endured but rather to be enjoyed, you knew what he meant. You could see it simply by watching him and listening to him.

When Hubert looked at the lives of black Americans in the '40s, he saw endurance and not enjoyment, and his heart insisted that it was time for Americans to walk forthrightly into the bright sunshine of human rights.

When Hubert looked at the young who could not get a good education, he saw endurance and not enjoyment. When Hubert saw old people in ill health, he saw endurance and not enjoyment. When Hubert saw middle-class people without jobs and decent homes, he saw endurance and not enjoyment.

Hubert was criticized for proclaiming the politics of joy. But he knew that joy is essential to us and is not frivolous. He loved to point out that ours is the only nation in the world to officially declare the pursuit of happiness as a national goal. But he was also a sentimental man and that was part of his life, too. He cried in public and without embarrassment. In his last major speech in his beloved Minnesota, he wiped tears from his eyes and said, "A man without tears is a man without a heart." If he cried often, it was not for himself, but for others.

Above all, Hubert was a man with a good heart. And on this sad day, it would be good for us to recall Shakespeare's words: "A good leg will fall. A straight back will stoop. A black beard will turn white. A curled pate will grow bald. A fair face will wither. A full eye will wax hollow. But a good heart is the sun and the moon. Or rather the sun and not the moon, for it shines bright and never changes, but keeps its course truly." Hubert's heart kept its course truly.

He taught us all how to hope and how to love, how to win and how to lose, he taught us how to live and, finally, he taught us how to die.

APPENDIX

BIOGRAPHICAL NOTES

BACON, WALLACE ALGER (1914-). Born, Bad Axe, Michigan; A.B., Albion College, 1935; M.A., University of Michigan, 1936; Ph.D., 1940; Lloyd Fellow, University of Michigan, 1940-41; instructor, Department of English, 1941-42, 1946-47; assistant professor of English and Speech, Northwestern University, 1947-50; associate professor, 1950-55; professor, 1955- ; chairman, department of interpretation, School of Speech, 1947- ; Rockefeller Foundation fellow, 1948-49; Ford Foundation fellow, 1954-55; Fulbright lecturer, University of Philippines, 1961-62; Fulbright-Hays lecturer, 1964-65; winner, Golden Anniversary Prize Fund (SCA), 1965, 1974; captain, AUS, 1942-46; Legion of Merit; author, *Savonarola,* 1950; (editor) *William Warner's Syrinx,* 1950; (coauthor) *Literature as Experience,* 1959; (coeditor) *Literature for Interpretation,* 1961; (coauthor) *The Art of Oral Interpretation,* 1965; *The Art of Interpretation,* 1966, 1972; (coauthor) *Spoken English,* 1962; *Oral Interpretation and Teaching of Literature in Secondary Schools,* 1974; president, Speech Communication Association, 1977; member, Phi Beta Kappa, Delta Sigma Rho, Theta Alpha Phi.

CALIFANO, JOSEPH ANTHONY, JR. (1931-). Born, Brooklyn, New York; A.B., Holy Cross College, 1952; LL.B., magna cum laude, Harvard University, 1955; admitted to N.Y. bar, 1955; with Dewey, Ballantine, Bushby, Palmer and Wood, New York City, 1958-61; special assistant to general counsel, Department of Defense, 1961-62; special assistant to Secretary of Army, 1962-63; general counsel, Department of Army, 1963-64; special assistant to Secretary of Defense and Deputy Secretary of Defense, 1964-65; special assistant to President Johnson, 1965-69; member of Arnold and Fortas, Washington, D.C., 1969-71; partner, Williams, Connolly and Califano, Washington, 1971-76; Secretary of Department of Health, Education and Welfare, 1977- ; lieutenant, USNR, 1955-58; author, *The Student Revolution: A Global Confrontation* (1969), *A Presidential Nation* (1975). (See also *Current Biography: June 1977.*)

CARPENTER, LIZ (Elizabeth Sutherland Carpenter) (1920-). Born, Salaso, Texas; B. Jour., University of Texas, 1942; reporter, United Press, Philadelphia, 1944-45; proprietor with husband of news bureau, Washington, D.C., 1945-61; executive assistant to Vice President Lyndon B. Johnson, 1961-63; press secretary to Lady Bird Johnson, 1963-69; policy council of National Women's Political Caucus, 1971- ; president, Women's National Press, 1954-55; presently cochairman ERAmerica; author, *Ruffles and Flourishes* (1970).

CARTER, JIMMY (James Earl Carter, Jr.) (1924-). Born, Plains, Georgia; student, Georgia Southwestern University, 1941-42; Georgia Institute of Technology, 1942-43; B.S., US Naval Academy, 1946; postgraduate instruction, nuclear physics, Union College, 1952; US Navy, 1947-53, advancing through grades to lieutenant commander; resigned 1953; farmer, warehouseman, 1953-77; served two terms in Georgia senate (Democrat), 1962-66 (voted most effective member); governor, 1971-74; chairman, Democratic National Campaign Committee, 1974; elected President, 1976; inaugurated, January 20, 1977; past president, Georgia Planning Association; first chairman, West Central Georgia Planning and Development Commission; former chairman, Sumter County Board of Education; district governor, Lions International; state chairman, March of Dimes; author, *Why Not the Best*, 1975. (See also *Current Biography: November 1977*.)

COLES, ROBERT MARTIN (1929-). Born, Boston, Massachusetts; A.B., Harvard University, 1950; M.D., Columbia University, College of Physicians and Surgeons, 1954; teaching fellow in psychiatry, Harvard Medical School, 1955-58; chief, neuropsychiatric service, USAF, Keesler Hospital, Biloxi, Mississippi, 1958-60; research psychiatrist, Southern Regional Council, 1961-63; consultant to the Council, 1965- ; consultant to Appalachian Volunteers, 1965- ; research psychiatrist, Harvard University Health Services, 1975- ; Phi Beta Kappa; awards, Ralph Waldo Emerson Award of Phi Beta Kappa (1967), Anisfield-Wolf Award in Race Relations of the *Saturday Review* (1968), Hofheimer Prize of American Psychiatric Association (1968), McAlpin Medal of the National Association of Mental Health (1972), Weatherford Prize of Berea College and the Council of Southern Mountains (1973), Lillian Smith Award of the Southern Regional Council (1973) and the Pulitzer Prize (1973); author of over twenty-five books including *Children of Crisis*, 5 volumes (1968, 1972), *Erik H. Erikson: The Growth of His Work* (1970), *The Middle Americans* (1971), *A Farewell to the South* (1972), *The Old Ones of New Mexico* (1973), *Irony in the Mind's Life* (1974), *The Knack of Survival in America* (1975), *The Mind's Fate* (1975); author of over five hundred articles, reviews, and monographs; contributing editor, *New Republic;*

editorial boards of *American Scholar, Contemporary Psychoanalysis, Child Psychiatry,* and *Human Development.* (See also *Current Biography: November 1969.*)

Duffey, Joseph Daniel (1932-). Born, Huntington, West Virginia; A.B., Marshall University, 1954; B.D., Andover Newton Theological School, 1957; S.T.M., Yale University, 1963; Ph.D., Hartford Seminary, 1969; ordained to ministry, Congregational Church; minister, First Congregational Church (now the United Church of Christ), Danvers, Mass., 1957-60; assistant professor, Hartford Seminary Foundation, 1960-64; unsuccessful Democratic candidate in Connecticut election for US Senate, 1970; adjunct professor Yale University and Fellow, Calhoun College, 1971-73; chief administrative officer, American Association of University Professors, 1974-77; chairman, Committee on Urban Renewal, Greater Hartford Community Council, 1962-64; board member, John F. Kennedy Center for the Performing Arts, Woodrow Wilson International Center For Scholars, and the East-West Center; US Assistant Secretary of State for Education, 1977; chairman, National Endowment for the Humanities, 1977- ; chairman, Federal Council of the Arts and Humanities, 1977- . (See also *Current Biography: March 1971.*)

Goldberg, Arthur Joseph (1908-). Born, Chicago, Illinois; B.S.L., Northwestern University, 1929; J.D., summa cum laude, 1929; recipient of twenty-four honorary degrees; admitted to Illinois bar, 1929; private practice, Chicago, 1929-48; partner in Goldberg, Devoe, Shadur and Mikva, Chicago, 1945-61; US Secretary of Labor, 1961-62; associate justice, US Supreme Court, 1962-65; US representative to UN, 1965-68; partner, Paul, Weiss, Goldberg, Rifkind, Wharton, and Garrison, New York, 1968-71; private practice of law, Washington, D.C., 1971- ; visiting professor of law, Princeton University, 1968-69; Columbia University, 1969-70; American University, 1972-73; Hastings College of Law, 1974- ; US Ambassador-at-Large and chairman of US Delegation to the Conference on Security and Cooperation in Europe (CSCE), September, 1977- ; OSS, 1942-43; captain to major AUS, 1942-44; author: *AFL-CIO Labor United* (1956), *Defenses Of Freedom* (1966), *Equal Justice: The Warren Era of the Supreme Court* (1972); contributor of numerous articles and reviews to law journals; member of Order of Coif. (See also *Current Biography: July 1961.*)

Hatch, Orrin Grant (1934-). Born, Homestead Park, Pa.; B.S., Brigham Young University, 1959; LL.B., University of Pittsburgh, 1962; admitted to Pennsylvania bar, 1963; senior partner, Hatch & Plumb, Salt Lake City, Utah; bishop, Church of Jesus Christ of Latter-Day Saints; US Senate (Republican, Utah) 1977- .

HAYAKAWA, SAMUEL ICHIYE (1906-). Born, Vancouver, B.C., Canada; B.A., University of Manitoba, 1927; M.A., McGill University, 1928; Ph.D., University of Wisconsin, 1935; naturalized US citizen, 1954; instructor, University of Wisconsin, 1936-39; instructor to associate professor, Illinois Institute of Technology, 1939-47; lecturer, University of Chicago, 1950-55; professor, San Francisco State College, 1955-68; president, 1968-73; author, *Language in Action* (1939); *Language in Thought and Action* (1949; 4th ed., 1977); *Language, Meaning and Maturity* (1954); *Our Language and Our Personality* (1963); editor, *ETC.*, 1943-70; US Senate (Republican, California), 1977- (See also *Current Biography: January 1977.*)

HUMPHREY, HUBERT HORATIO, JR. (1911-1977). Born, Wallace, South Dakota; A.B., University of Minnesota, 1939; M.A.; Louisiana State University, 1940; honorary degrees from forty colleges and universities; state director, War Production Training, 1942; assistant director, War Manpower Commission, 1943; visiting professor, Macalester College, 1943-44; professor, 1969-70; mayor, Minneapolis, 1945-48; US Senate (Democrat, Minnesota), 1948-64, 1971-77; US Vice President, 1965-69; Democratic nominee for President, 1968; author: *Cause Is Mankind* (1964), *Political Philosophy of the New Deal* (1970), *Young America in the New World* (1971), *School Desegregation* (ed.) (1964); member of Phi Beta Kappa and Delta Sigma Rho. (See also *Current Biography: April 1966.*)

MCGILL, WILLIAM JAMES (1922-). Born, New York City; A.B., Fordham College, 1943; M.A., 1947; Ph.D., Harvard University, 1953; instructor, Fordham University, 1947-48; teaching fellow, Harvard University, 1949-50; instructor, Boston College, 1950-51; staff member, Lincoln Laboratory (MIT), 1951-54; assistant professor, Massachusetts Institute of Technology, 1954-56; assistant professor, Columbia University, 1956-58; associate professor, 1958-60; professor, 1960-65; professor, University of California, San Diego, 1965-68; chancellor, 1968-70; president, Columbia University, 1970- ; fellow, American Association for the Advancement of Science, 1963; American Psychological Association, 1967; board of trustees, Psychometric Society, 1967- ; associate editor, *Journal of Mathematical Psychology,* 1964- , *Perception and Psychophysics,* 1966-70; consulting editor, *Psychological Bulletin,* 1966-70; *Psychometrika,* 1965-70; published over 35 studies and reviews; member, Phi Beta Kappa, Sigma Xi; Achievement Award of Fordham University, 1968. (See also *Current Biography: June 1971.*)

McGraw, Harold Whittlesey, Jr. (1918-). Born, Brooklyn, New York; A.B., Princeton University, 1940; G. M. Basford Advertising Agency, 1940-41; Brentano's Bookstores, Inc., 1946; McGraw-Hill Book Company, Inc., 1947- ; senior vice president, 1961-68; president, 1968-74; chief executive officer, 1974- ; president, Princeton University Press; USAAF., 1941-45.

McIntyre, Thomas James (1915-). Born, Laconia, New Hampshire; B.A., Dartmouth College, 1937; LL.B., Boston University, 1940; honorary degrees, Belknap College, University of New Hampshire, Nathaniel Hawthorne College, and Dartmouth College; practiced law, 1946-67; mayor, 1949-51, city solicitor, 1953, Laconia, N.H.; AUS, 1942-46, four battle stars, Combat Infantry Badge, Bronze Star with oakleaf cluster for meritorious achievement; retired as major; US Senate (Democrat, New Hampshire), 1963- . (See also *Current Biography: November 1963.*)

Mathias, Charles McCurdy, Jr. (1922-). Born, Frederick, Maryland; US Navy, 1942-46; B.A., Haverford College, 1944; LL.B., University of Maryland, 1949; partner, Mathias, Mathias & Michel, Frederick, 1949-53; assistant attorney general of Maryland, 1953-54; city attorney, Frederick, 1954-59; member, House of Delegates, Maryland, 1958; partner, Niles, Barton, Markell and Gans, Baltimore, 1960- ; member, US House of Representatives (Republican, Maryland), 1961-67; US Senate, 1968- . (See also *Current Biography: December 1972.*)

Mondale, Walter Frederick (1928-). Born, Ceylon, Minnesota; B.A., cum laude, University of Minnesota, 1951; LL.B., 1956; admitted to Minnesota bar, 1956; private practice of law, 1956-60; attorney general, state of Minnesota, 1960-64; US Senate (Democrat, Minnesota), 1964-76; AUS, 1951-53; US Vice President, 1977- . (See also *Current Biography: May 1978.*)

Moynihan, Daniel Patrick (1927-). Born, Tulsa, Oklahoma; B.A. cum laude, Tufts University, 1948; M.A., 1949; Ph.D., Fletcher School of Law and Diplomacy, 1961; LL.D., St. Louis University, 1968; Fulbright fellow, London (England) School of Economics and Political Science, 1950-51; special assistant to US Secretary of Labor, 1961-62; executive assistant, 1962-63; Assistant Secretary of Labor, 1963-65; director, Joint Center Urban Studies, Massachusetts Institute of Technology and Harvard University, 1966-69; professor, education and urban politics, senior member, Kennedy School of Government, Harvard University, 1966-73; assistant for urban affairs to President of United States, 1969-70; counselor to President Nixon, member of cabinet, 1971-73; US ambassador to India, 1973-75; US ambassador to United Nations, 1975-76; US Senate (Democrat, New York), 1977- ; USNR, 1944-47; member, American Academy of Arts and Sciences; numerous committees, including New York State Democratic Convention, 1958-60; member, New York State delegation, Democratic National Convention, 1960; vice chairman, Woodrow Wilson International Center for Scholars, 1971- ; author, *Maximum Feasible Misunderstanding,* 1969; *Beyond the Melting Pot* (with Nathan Glazer), 1963. (See also *Current Biography: February 1968.*)

ROOT, TRENT C., JR. (1926-). Born, Temple, Texas; B.B.A., Texas Tech University, 1949; Texas Power and Light Company, 1949- ; test engineer, 1949-50; power consultant, 1950-51; local manager, Bonham, Texas, 1941-42; district manager, 1952-61; assistant to president, 1961-64; assistant vice president, 1964-68; vice president, 1968- ; 2nd lieutenant AAF, World War II.

RUSK, DEAN (1909-). Born, Cherokee County, Georgia; A.B,. magna cum laude, Davidson College, 1931; B.S., St. John's College, Oxford University (Rhodes scholar), 1933; M.A., 1934; LL.D., Mills College, 1948; other honorary degrees; associate professor of government, and dean, Mills College, 1934-40; assistant chief, Division of International Security Affairs, US Department of State, 1946; special assistant to Secretary of War, 1946-47; director, Office of United Nations Political Affairs, US Department of State, 1947-49; Assistant Secretary of State, February 1949; Deputy Under Secretary of State, 1949-50; Assistant Secretary of State, Far Eastern Affairs, 1950-51; Secretary of State, 1961-69; president, Rockefeller Foundation, 1952-60; Sibley Professor of International Law, University of Georgia, 1970- ; Legion of Merit; Phi Beta Kappa. (See also *Current Biography: July 1961.*)

SEVAREID, (ARNOLD) ERIC (1912-). Born, Velva, North Dakota; B.A., University of Minnesota, 1935; attended the London School of Economics and the Alliance in Paris; reporter and editor of the Paris edition of the New York *Herald Tribune,* 1938-39; worked in France with Edward R. Murrow, Columbia Broadcasting System, 1939-41; CBS News Bureau, Washington, D.C., 1941-43; war correspondent, in Asia, 1943-44; in Europe, 1944-45; CBS Washington Bureau, 1946-59; roving European correspondent, CBS, 1959-61; moderator, CBS telecasts of *Town*

Meeting of the World, The Great Challenge, Years of Crisis, and *Where We Stand;* CBS Evening News with Walter Cronkite from Washington, 1964-77; author, *Canoeing With the Cree* (1935), *Not So Wild a Dream* (1946), *In One Ear* (1952), *Small Sounds in the Night* (1956), *This Is Eric Sevareid* (1964), *Candidates, 1960* (1959); received numerous awards; past president, Radio Correspondents.

YALOW, ROSALYN SUSSMAN (1921-). Born, New York City, N.Y.; B.A., Hunter College, 1941; M.S., University of Illinois, 1942; Ph.D., 1945; assistant in physics, University of Illinois, 1941-43; instructor, 1944; assistant engineer, Federal Telecommunications Laboratory, New York City, 1945-46; lecturer and assistant professor, Hunter College, 1946-50; chief, Radio Immunoassay Reference Laboratory, Veterans Administration Hospital, 1969- ; chief, Nuclear Medical Service, 1970- ; senior medical investigator, 1972- ; research professor in the Department of Medicine, School of Medicine, at Mount Sinai of New York City, 1968-74; Middleton Award, 1960; Lilly Award, American Diabetes Association, 1961; Federation Women's Award, 1961; Van Slyke Award, American Association of Clinical Chemistry Endocrine Society, 1972; Gairdner Foundation International Award, 1971; A. Cressy Morrison Award of New York Academy of Science 1975; Albion O. Bernstein Medical Award, Medical Society of New York, 1974; Nobel Prize for Physiology, 1977.

(824)

CUMULATIVE AUTHOR INDEX

1970-1971—1977-1978

A cumulative author index to the volumes of REPRESENTATIVE AMERICAN SPEECHES for the years 1937-1938 through 1959-1960 appears in the 1959-1960 volume and for the years 1960-1961 through 1969-1970 in the 1969-1970 volume.